Tim Quinn
in an Exciting Adventure in Time and Space

Intro(spection)

When I first went to live in America I was given a pre Green Card that stated I was a RESIDENT ALIEN. No truer words have ever been writ. I remember feeling that way on my first day of school, and, years later, on being handed my first official Letter of Warning at Marvel Comics. I have encountered many appalling Earthlings in my time but also, luckily, many wonderful fellow aliens. All in all it has been a laugh a minute and I'm still not dead on most days. I hope the following tale is readable and brings a few pictures to mind…

Published 2023 First Edition
NEW HAVEN PUBLISHING LTD
www.newhavenpublishingltd.com
newhavenpublishing@gmail.com

Cover Design © Tim Quinn

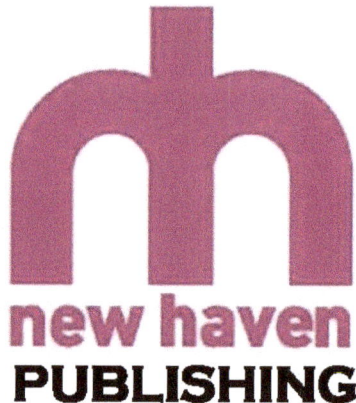

new haven
PUBLISHING

DEDICATION

To Jane, my wife, my life

Content

ARGH!

"ARGH!" My mother always swore that was my very first word on planet Earth. Hardly a wonder when you consider what my first sight must have been. I was born on Monday the 21st of September 1953 at 6:00am in Park House nursing home in Liverpool. The mini hospital was run and staffed by nuns. That's nuns of the period, not today's bright and trendy looking nuns. So my very first sight on planet Earth was of a period nun in the full black habit, cosh-rosary, and cowl, complete with surgical face-mask. "ARGH!" indeed.

For this was Liverpool at the midpoint of the Twentieth Century. Priests, nuns and, worst of all, Irish Christian Brothers roamed the streets freely with a religious system straight out of the Middle Ages. "Thou shalt not..." was the Golden Rule. Is it any wonder I took to reading The Beano at the earliest opportunity? Liverpool in the mid Fifties was a city designed by Victorian architects and Adolf Hitler. Herman Goering to be precise. His Luftwaffe had cut a swathe through the place, and ten years on from the blitz, overgrown bombsites had become part of the landscape. Together with the abandoned army camp, Fort Crosby, on the banks of the River Mersey, Liverpool was the perfect playground for this kid to grow up in. And things were abuzz. I was born in perfect time for Rock & Roll and the plethora of naughty kids that exploded from Scottish weekly comic books during the Fifties. Menaces, Perils, Smashers, Minxes, Dodgers and Bash Street Kids led the revolution against authority of all kinds. Peashooters and bricks aimed at the back of a teacher's head made us see exactly how ridiculous the pomposity of the established order really was. Satire started in the comics, years before David Frost and co picked up on it.

Oddly, the first 2 years of my life are a complete blank. Something so bloody awful must have been happening to me on a daily basis that I have removed all memories from my brain simply to stay sane(ish). I see from history books that Everest was conquered and Queen Elizabeth II was crowned, giving birth to television aerials popping up on rooftops across the land during this amnesiac time.

One thing I do know is that I was named after a comic book character. Yes, my Mum had loved Tiger Tim and the Bruin Boys in the *Rainbow* comic when she was growing up in the Twenties, and so when it came to name her favourite child there was only one name to choose. I guess that kind of set things in motion for my future. It helped that I had been born striped. Yes, I said striped. Doctors and nurses blamed it on my mother's wartime diet. Powdered eggs and Spam. Well, that was their theory but there I was covered in bright stripes. After her initial shock and horror, Mum found it quite cute and always referred to me as her little Tiger Tim. Sadly, the stripes faded after the first few months before the Quinn's could have made a fortune selling me to Barnum & Bailey's Touring Freak Show.

My very earliest memory is of my Mum handing me a stick of charcoal and telling me to go and draw on my bedroom wall. I was two years and eleven months of age and we had just that day moved into our first home, a huge rambling Victorian house twenty minutes from the centre of Liverpool. As luck would have it, I drew a hardboiled egg, which with a bit of added scribble and a smiley face passed as a recognizable hedgehog. I had a character that I could start telling stories about. And start telling stories I did. It was a big bedroom with huge walls. As befits the 1950's, the first story I told in 5 pictures had the hedgehog (who I named Tim…I didn't know many names at that age) finding a space rocket in his back garden. Luckily, it was the 1950's because space rockets were easy to draw then being simple cigar-shapes with fins and portholes rather than the complicated monstrosities post Star Wars. I remember that I added a letter-slot in the front door of the rocket so the inhabitants could receive their daily mail. Tim climbed aboard, traveled across space and landed on the moon where he found he could leap tall distances in a single bound. That was it. If there are any movie producers reading this, the rights are still available. Hey, I was only 2 and a bit!

Schooldays – What can I say? I found the majority of teachers daft although I am eternally grateful to Sisters Monica and Ethelreda at the Ursuline Convent for helping me crack the code of Riting and Reading. And one wonderful form teacher I had for 2 years at The Mount. Mr Fitzgerald turned his whole class into readers by introducing us to Conan Doyle's 'The Lost World'. Still a favourite book, and I can still hear Mr Fitzgerald's accent reading Sir John Roxton's part. The rest of the teachers left something to be desired. The only thing they inspired me to do was play truant and look forward to turning 16 so I could get the hell out of Limbo. For this was a Catholic school where we were encouraged to look ahead at all times to Death, when we would move over to one of 3 places: Limbo, Purgatory or Hell. I was age six when they dropped that one on me, and seven when I decided they were all nutters. It was after my first (and last) confession. I didn't have a clue what to put up as my sin of the day so when the priest asked me to confess my sins I replied: "I didn't take my medicine today." I was on a course of Minadex to promote growth in 7 year-olds. The priest didn't skip a beat: "Say 2 Hail Mary's and an Our Father and I absolve you of the sin of not taking your medicine." Kind of like the Get Out of Jail Free Card in Monopoly. And that was it with me and religion. And school.

I found I had a knack for looking out of the classroom window and imagining all sorts of stories as I wandered freely with my dog Rags around Liverpool. There were two other boys in my class with the same talent. At age 10 we teamed-up to produce a weekly comic to sell to our classmates. I came up with the title, The Banger, and the main character, Wat Why, a dog. This was in 1963, a time way before photocopiers so turning out copies of our work was a pain in the neck after the initial enthusiasm for the project wore off. We did 3 issues in all with

12 pages in each edition. I remember that the very final page showed we had already moved on. It was 8 empty panels laid out in typical comic book format with the title: YOUR CHANCE TO MAKE YOUR OWN COMIC STRIP!

Comics were a huge part of my life by this time. What a great period to grow up in. Every week the newsagent's shelf groaned and sagged under the sheer weight of the comic weeklies. Such a variety of stories exploded from the pages of titles like Lion, Valiant, TV Express, Buster, and The New Hotspur. On one page you would have an adventure set on Mars followed by stories in the Wild West, under the ocean, in deepest jungle, highest mountain, prehistory, and public school. Robots, spacemen, cowboys, pirates, schoolboys, detectives, and explorers became my pals. Over in the funnies, Oor Wullie and The Broons bi-annual books became my favourites. Written in the thickest Scottish dialect, which I still drop into on occasion, these glorious books captured exactly what it was like to be a boy in the Twentieth Century.

And then there were the American comic books. What a joy to find the odd newsagent who had the imports displayed on a whizzy comic book rack featuring the best from so many US publishers. Dell, DC, Harvey, Archie, Gold Key, Atlas, and then…Marvel Pop Art Productions! And how lucky was I? We had let the top floor of our house to an American family. The Dad was over here working for the US Air Force out of Burtonwood base in Liverpool. He would take brother Mike and I onto the base to see the planes and, even better, have a rummage through the PX where they sold American comics and candy. Tootsie Rolls and Dime bars, no less, but all the very latest comics hot off the press. Ohh…the excitement!

I wouldn't describe myself as a violent boy although the list of weapons in my armoury might make you think otherwise. Colt pistols and holster with silver Lone Ranger bullets, a luger, Captain Cutlass's very own cap pistol, a machine gun with realistic sound, various spud guns, peashooter, catapult, Buffalo Bill rifle, Dan Dare's ray gun, and a bloody great sheaf knife strapped to my thigh over my shorts and school blazer and cap.

On top of this I had legions of toy soldiers that I would slaughter daily in battles across my bedroom floor. This was an army like no other with US Civil War soldiers fighting alongside WW1 and WW2 Nazis, Tommies, Japanese kamikaze pilots and Robin Hood and his Merry Men. A real war to end all wars.

My grandfather on Mum's side had already coloured my view of war long before John Lennon suggested giving peace a chance. Pop, as we called him, had got off to a bad start in life by being born just at the right time to have to fight in 2 world wars. He never forgave the political bastards who sent his generation into Hell. Fooled by the jingoistic media of the day, he joined the Royal Flying Corps by lying about his age when he was just 15. He soon fell out with his so-called superior officer who referred to him as a "little shit". Not a smart thing to do with Pop. One grim day he snapped and broke the officer's nose. "I can still hear the crack," he would beam whenever recounting the tale during my childhood. Amazingly he wasn't shot but rather court-martialled and sent into the military in the trenches, where his British made gasmask proved faulty and he inhaled a near lethal dose of mustard gas which sent him back to Blighty days before his troop were shot to bits. During the early Sixties when it looked as though WW3 was on its way, he tried to calm any fears I might have by saying that he would shoot me in both feet rather than let me be called up. As I was only about 8 or 9 years of age at the time I had certain reservations about this. The top floor of Pop's house was a real armoury containing allsorts he had picked up during the 2 wars. Machine guns, rifles, pistols, bullets by the ton, grenades, bayonets, a bazooka, and even a Samurai sword! Brother Mike and I loved getting togged up with all this real weaponry and battling it out round the house. I remember seeing a grenade come bouncing down the staircase towards me during one major skirmish. Tis a wonder we are both still here.

We got our telly in 1960, in perfect timing for Gerry Anderson's Tex Tucker in Four Feather Falls. As puppet shows go, it was a mighty leap from the wetter-than-wet Torchy the Battery Boy. I

13

was hooked from episode 1 at the cast of highly likeable characters, a staple of Anderson's series. I was already a cowboy before FFF. I don't think there was a day of the week without a Western series on the TV. Cheyene, Bronco Laine, Tenderfoot, Laramie, Bonanza, The Lone Ranger, Hoppalong Cassidy, Rawhide, Wagon Train, The Rifleman … the list was endless. Once home from school, off would come the cap and blazer to be replaced by Davy Crockett's coonskin hat or a full Sioux Chief feathered headdress as I would hunt for palefaces or outlaws out in the garden. This is how West Liverpool was won. There was one cowboy I couldn't stand though. He even had a full-page colour strip on the back of TV Comic. This was the original Milky Bar Kid. Specky little git. Didn't like his chocolate bar and didn't like him. Oddly, 50+ years on, the thought of him still gets my goat. Time to let it go. I thought he was a waste of space in TV Comic even though he had only replaced the equally dreadful weekly story about The Ladybird Adventurers, which was an advertisement for Woolworth's own kids' clothing line.

Yes, telly was good. There was an air of experimentation about it back then. Even though there were only two channels and programming from 5-midnight, they crammed a lot in. Westerns, detectives, plays, comedy, variety, pop, and some pretty wacky cartoons such as Foo-Foo & Go-Go, and Bulwinkle & Rocky. The Granada TV area was really cooking. Their local news shows, People & Places, and Scene at 6:60, were run by real journalists (remember them?) with a flair for presenting, news, and entertainment. They were fun shows to watch and gave me a pull to work in TV at some point in my life. What a difference today's dreary local news shows are. You could be anywhere in the country and they are all the same. Luckily I'm not one to moan.

And then there was music. Oh yes. I was growing up in Liverpool, you see, in the Fifties and early Sixties. Music was everywhere, especially in our house. Mum and Dad bought our 3D Radiogram in 1957. Its sound filled the house with my parents' varied choice in music. Beethoven, Mozart, Liszt,

Strauss, Deanna Durbin, Glen Miller, Roaring Twenties Jazz Age hits, bloody John McCormack, Calypso, Harry Belafonte, and the Beverley Sisters. My very first record was the Jack & Jill Party Record from 1957. It was advertised in my Jack & Jill weekly and featured all the characters from the comic attending a party. It was one of those cardboard records that were big at the time. It is pinned to the office wall behind me as I type, signed by Rolf Harris (many years later when I was on his TV show) who did all the voices.

It was 1962 when I started buying my own records. First up was the James Bond Theme by the John Barry Seven followed by Dance On by The Shadows. Both instrumentals get me to this day. Talk about a groove going on. Great start to the collection that now fills a whole room of my house, but back then something dreadful happened. I bought my first LP. Cliff Richard & The Shadows in The Young Ones. Now keep in mind this was one hell of an expense for a boy on pocket money. Thirty-two shillings and sixpence. That's a lot of comic books. And it was bloody dreadful, crammed full of the ghastly kind of tunes that filled out a pop movie of the period. I swore I would never buy another LP. Thanks, Cliff. And then I heard Please, Please Me. It stopped me in my tracks as I came into my house from an afternoon's playing in the snow and ice on one of the coldest Winter's since records began. It was Sunday 20th January 1963. I marked it in my Enid Blyton Diary. Everything changed for me that day. That was the moment the Sixties truly began. I stood there in the kitchen transfixed by the radio. Nothing had ever sounded like that. They say nothing is Black & White. That record was. I remember thinking that I was glad I was in my tat – torn jeans and baggy ripped sweater. I knew whoever was making this sound would be dressed like this. So it was quite a surprise a week or so later when I saw my first photograph of The Beatles. They were in suits! Even so, there was something so coolly tat about those faces and that hair. By then I'd bought the single and loved both A and B sides. So by the time they released their first LP a couple of months later I was ready to make that gamble. I'd been let down by Cliff but this was The Beatles, and guess what? They came from Liverpool. Even so, it was with a little trepidation that I dropped the stylus on Side 1 for the first play. That fear was instantly kicked out by the countdown to I Saw Her Standing There: "One, Two, Three, Four…" Every track grabbed me in a different way, right through to the cheer of triumph at the end of Side 2's Twist & Shout. Cosmic, Gamma Powered music. The Beatles. I do believe they have come up in conversation every day since. Bigger on the Inside than Jesus? I should say so!

Love – SHOUT IT!

AT AGE 8 I FELL IN LOVE FOR THE FIRST TIME WITH DUSTY SPRINGFIELD AFTER SEEING HER WITH HER BAND THE SPRINGFIELDS AT THE LIVERPOOL EMPIRE THEATRE. SHE WAS 24 AT THE TIME AND THE AGE DIFFERENCE GOT IN THE WAY OF OUR ROMANCE. THAT AND THE FACT THAT SHE WAS A LESBIAN AND I WASN'T.

AT AGE ELEVEN AND A HALF I FELL IN LOVE FOR THE SECOND TIME WITH LADY PENELOPE IN THE PAGES OF TV21 COMIC. I HAD NO PROBLEM WITH THE AGE DIFFERENCE OR THE FACT THAT SHE WAS A PUPPET, BUT IT WAS NOT TO BE.

Beatles, Books & Telly

By August of 1963 The Beatles were exploding in every direction. I now had their first three singles and first LP together with a bedroom full of press cuttings. What could be better? I'll tell you what could be better. Mum coming into my room with tickets for brother Mike and I to see the boys live at the Odeon Cinema up the railway track in Southport. Yes, LIVE! Not on screen but LIVE! I love my mother! And what a day Monday 26th August 1963 turned out to be. Three great bands on the bill: The Fourmost, Gerry and the Pacemakers and The Beatles. Not bad for 8/6d! We got there early to hang around the Stage Door. No Fabs spotted but I did get Brian O'Hara of The Fourmost's autograph and a tack out of his Chelsea Boot. The show itself was … Fab, what else?! I have no words to describe it other than that the rhythm and beat of that show is still vibrating through my solar system. We had good seats up front and I do remember that George Harrison had really plastered on the make-up about a yard thick. Cool look! I also remember that when The Beatles took the stage the whole cinema erupted. I was yelling for Ringo until the girl in front of me turned round with a face of thunder and roared: "SHURRUP!" Obviously a Pete Best fan.

Between comics and music and telly, books were a big part of my life from Year Dot. Mum had been a librarian until Hitler had bombed her library. That was the way she told it so I always pictured the man himself at the controls of the Fuhrer Bomber, looking down on Merseyside and saying: "There! That's the library we must destroy. Bombs away!" Despite that old bastard, Mum brought books into my life from an early age and I have always loved the feel, smell, sight, and very paper of books. It was a Big Deal day when Mum took me to get my first Library Card. Still got it, of course. The very first book I read from cover to cover was Noddy and the Magic Rubber, which gives some qualms to my American friends, particularly when I then tell them that I won a Blue Peter badge in 1964. The badge was for sending in a 'very interesting idea for our programme'. I have no idea what that idea was but I am delighted that it was very interesting. Blue Peter was the BBC's finest children's magazine programme, dropping seeds of interest in a million subjects into kids' heads for over 50 years. Noddy was the creation of Enid Blyton, the finest writer for children ever! I went on to read shelf-loads of her books through my childhood. I've yet to come down from the Magic Faraway Tree.

As well as TV Westerns, I also loved the various detective series of the Sixties. The Avengers (non-Mighty), 77 Sunset Strip, Danger Man, but especially The Prisoner. This show was so in tune with the times, and even had The Beatles All You Need is Love playing in the final episode. During the school summer holidays in '68, I got a call from my elder brother Mike. He had got himself a job in The Village, no less. Turns out The Prisoner's prison was not in some faraway exotic land but rather in North Wales at a place called Portmeirion. Mike told me to pack my bags and come on down as he had organized a summer job for me in the village itself! It is a truly breathtaking place. A real escape from planet Earth. The very air is different somehow to anywhere else. I was given a chalet, just like No. 6's, all meals and £7.00 a week for my services as a dogsbody. I did stuff. Dishes in the hotel kitchen, light bulbs in the chalets, litter out of the ponds. At 6pm every night, the general public were turfed out and the Village became mine. I bought a tinny record player and soon Donovan, the Lovin' Spoonful, and the Incredible String Band were adding to the atmosphere. No small thanks to my elder brother, a cloud of marijuana smoke hovered over Portmeirion that Summer. He was keen to get me converted to the weed. We sat and watched a sunrise one morning. Mike lovingly rolling a joint, took a huge drag, closed his eyes and handed it to me. I looked at the sunrise over the Village and then back to him with his eyes closed missing everything. It was one of those turning points. He could keep his joint. I have to say that he has, and very happily too. He was last seen heading into the Back of Beyond in the outback of Australia where he joined a tribe of Aborigines. The funny thing is that back then everybody always made the mistake of thinking I was the stoned one. Mike had a straighter look. A look he has since lost. It was during this summer that I wrote my first (and last) poem. Inspired by the setting and Donovan, the opening line ran, 'The multi-coloured jester ran through the rain, his smile a disguise for 1,000 years of pain…' Exactly. Hey, don't blame me. It was the Sixties and there was a dope cloud hovering.

Meanwhile, back at school, I encountered the Smarmy Teacher. I would enter the classroom and he would stop me in my tracks with the question:

ST: What are you, Quinn?
Me: I don't know. What am I, sir?
ST: You're a clown, Quinn, a clown. What are you?
Me: I'm a clown, sir. A clown.

Now fair enough, life must be pretty crappy for teachers like that and I suppose they must take their perks where they can, but even so. This wasn't a one-off occasion. It was every bloody lesson. Enough to give you a complex…if you didn't like clowns, that is. Unfortunately for ST, I did like clowns. Not the awful children's entertainer type who put on a red nose and thought they were immediately comic. No, not them but the real clowns. A tremendous moment in my life had been the day Coco the Clown visited my class back when I was a six year-old. He was promoting road safety and telling us how to look left, look right and look left again. Now Coco was a real clown with a rich history in the circus. Even more wonderful for me was that he was a character in my weekly TV Comic where he featured in a beautifully drawn strip. The moment he walked into my classroom was the moment that I realized for sure that comic book characters are real. So I have kind of always had a thing

20

for real clowns. Calling me one didn't rate high on the punishment scale. The fact was though that I wasn't a clown in class. I was the semi-conscious guy at the back looking out the window. But, as things turned out, I probably have that teacher to thank for my life turning out as it has.

Circus Boy

I left school at the end of the Sixties without a clue as to my future. The advice I'd been given by the school Careers Officer went like this:

CO: What are your interests?
Me: I like music, drawing and writing.
CO: Drawing, eh?
Me: Yeah, I particularly like comic book art.
CO: Hmm. What you should do is go to Lewis's department store and see if they need somebody to write out the price tags that go in the shop windows.

That was it. The extent of advice for a life in the Arts from my old school. Thank you. Very insightful. I walked out of the room thinking, what a git. Not that I had any other ideas in my head. However, the morning after I left school I was asked by my elder brother just what I hoped to do now. I told him that I just wanted to do something to prove I was alive. Not a bad plan really. After saying this, my old teacher's clown liturgy came to mind. On a whim, I packed a bag with undies and socks and a clean shirt and jeans, and took off for the coach station. I bought a one-way ticket up coast to Blackpool, where I walked from the station to the tower itself. Finding the Stage Door to the Blackpool Tower Circus, I knocked. And knocked again. After a pause it was opened by one of the most famous faces from the circus world. Charlie Cairoli had been a mainstay of BTC for nearly 40 years as head clown. And here he was in full make-up complete with bowler hat, looking me up and down. "What do you want?" he asked. "Any jobs going?" He looked me in the eye for a full minute of silence before opening the door further and nodding for me to enter. "Follow me," he said, leading the way to his dressing room. He sat me down in front of a mirror and proceeded to apply all sorts of slop to my face. A wig and jolly clothes were added. And so it was that 24 hours after leaving school I made my debut as a clown alongside Charlie and his troupe in the ring of the Blackpool Tower Circus to an audience of what seemed like thousands. My job was to throw buckets of water in the direction of Charlie but to make sure I missed with everyone. I would then have paste and water thrown at me and I must make sure that each bucket hit me. It did. Those clowns were good. Another part of my job was to act as Ringboy (I hope they have changed that title by now), a virtual stagehand, carrying and rolling props in and out of the ring. As most of the props would have elephants or tigers standing on them they were a dead weight and you had to find a way to carry or spin them into the ring double-quick so as not to slow down the whole show which ran at breakneck speed. For the first few weeks I was also the guy with a bucket who had to race into the ring to clean up if the elephants left anything in their wake. They usually did. All teen self-consciousness left me forever after the first week of doing this.

Charlie was a funny guy. I don't think I ever saw him smile. He would always come and stand beside me during the flying trapeze act. Each performance he would say exactly the same thing: "I only watch this in case one of them falls." He would then tut in disappointment at the end of each act that the trapeze artist survived.

In an attempt to figure out who/what/why I was, I had decided to become a vegetarian on the coach ride up to Blackpool. Not as easy a task back then as it is today. There were no vegetarian meals to be found in stores so you had to figure it out yourself. As my job as clown/ringboy was pretty strenuous I had to figure it out swiftly as energy levels were all important. To begin with I would buy a chunk of cheese and a loaf of bread.

Very filling but… The lot of the circus animals was a miserable one. To see elephants and tigers being paraded round the ring to the squawks and screeches of the audience was a depressing sight. Behind the scenes the animals were kept in cramped conditions, which made my vegetarian sense tingle.

I'd booked into a seedy boarding house. My room was in the attic and I felt very lonely whenever I returned there. No emails. No mobile. No Facebook. No instant communication with the outside world. Just me. The boarding house had a bathroom that gave me the creeps. There was something in the bath. To this day I don't know what it was and nor do I want to know, but it kept me out the bath the entire time I was there. That could well be the reason I caught fleas at one point. Possibly from the circus or possibly from the boarding house. Itchy. Between shows I'd go and sit on the pier with my loaf of bread and watch the seagulls go by. I looked a little curly-headed innocent and consequently attracted the passing trade in nonces. They would come and sit next to me and gradually work their way closer up the bench until our legs would touch in what I guess they must have seen as a courting gesture. When this failed to get the hoped for response from me, they would pull out a wallet and flash the ten shilling notes within. I was very polite the first few times this happened and simply made my excuses and left. After a month or so though I hit upon a brilliant way to get out of this situation whenever it arose. I would shout in a really loud voice the words 'fuck' and 'off'. It worked a dream and I have applied it on many occasions since with equal success even though my nonce attracting days are long over.

One thing became clear as the months went on. I wasn't much of a clown. Yes, I could throw buckets of water and slop like the best of them but the Chaplin/Coco instinct was nowhere to be found in my genes. And so at the end of the season when Charlie Cairoli asked about my plans I answered truthfully, "Well I know I'm not a clown, despite what my teacher may have said." Charlie nodded in agreement. "This is true," he said. He then told me about an old Music Hall in Leeds and suggested I might find work backstage there for the panto season. I had no better idea, so, my circus and flea-ridden days behind me, I hitched a ride over to Leeds.

Good Old Days

Leeds was a fairly dour place to me back then. Keep in mind this is pre-Harvey Nicks days. It suited the phrase, it's grim up North. I found the theatre, The World Famous Leeds City Varieties Music Hall. There were two identical huge twins sitting in the box office, both with owl-like thick tin rim specs. They pointed my way to the Stage Door, down a tiny alleyway littered with dustbins and overflowing garbage. I walked through the door and found myself.

The City Varieties is definitely bigger on the inside. It was like stepping back in time to a world full of Dickensian characters. The theatre was over 200 years-old. It was mid-morning as I headed up a set of stairs, across the Green Room and up another three steps to the stage itself. The theatre was in darkness but I could hear somebody thirty-feet above me clambering around in the Fly gallery. He stuck his head over the rail and called down: "Yeah?" I called up: "Any jobs going?" A trail of fag ash descended from on high. "Wait!" he called. Minutes later he joined me on the stage, puffing and panting, fag still in mouth, ash all down his front, slicked back jet black hair, which I later found out to be coloured with boot polish. This was Wally, Stage Manager supreme. "Do you know how to work the limes?" he asked. I didn't even know what the limes were. "Be back here at two and I'll show you before the show begins at 2:30."

The limes were hardly brain surgery but still quite tricky to handle. Up in the gods was the Lime Box, a tiny booth for two spotlights operated by touching carbon rods and a boost of electricity. My fellow lime man was 'Old Pop' who looked as if he had been there since the theatre's opening night. The spotlights were of similar age. The show was Snow White and the Seven Dwarfs, which was advertised on the posters as WITH 7 REAL LIVE DWARFS! I guess this was as opposed to the dead variety other theatres featured. I found that Old Pop would sometimes doze off during the show. It tended to get very hot in the Lime Box and by the time you've seen the same show 50 times or more I could see his problem. There would be a splutter of carbon rods and his light would go out, literally.

For me it was a fun show and a most beautiful theatre. The same family, the Josephs, had run the place since before WW2. In my first week there while swecping out the attic I discovered a poster advertising the Eight Lancashire Lads imminent arrival at the theatre. Charlie Chaplin had been one of the lads. The place really hadn't changed a bit since Victorian times. The BBC were there regularly to film a long running TV series, The Good Old Days, which was basically a night in a Victorian music hall, starring a variety of entertainers from Arthur Askey, Ken Dodd, Charlie Drake, Albert Modley, Ted Ray and Bruce Forsyth to Frankie Vaughan. Everybody, including the audience, would dress in Victorian costume so that, apart from the TV cameras, it was like stepping back through time. I remember Lonnie Donegan doing a double-take when he saw me and saying: "I see you have come in disguise as Arlo Guthrie." Arlo and I did share a similar look at the time.

The BBC would turn up late on a Saturday night with two huge outside broadcast vans that filled the alley at the back of the theatre. We stagehands would strip down whatever show was currently running and carry in all the props and gear for The Good Old Days, setting up backcloths for each act. We would get out round 4am and be back for first rehearsal by 10 that morning. By this time the cameras would be in place. There were just three so as to not intrude too much on the Victorian atmosphere for the audience. One would be placed at the back of the stalls, another in a theatre box stage right, and the third at stalls right. I'm sure Dicky Howett would like to know the exact type of camera used so I will apply my technical knowledge here to say they were bloody great big ones. The dress rehearsal would take place at 6pm and the audience would be let in by 7:45pm for kick off at 9. As the series had already been running since the Fifties, it was very rare for anything to go wrong during the recording. The only overruns I remember were when Ken Dodd topped the bill and that was par for the course. The audience would usually be out no later than 10:45pm while we stage crew did the reverse of the previous night, stripping The Good Old Days and resetting for Monday's show. All fun and all very exciting.

One incident comes to mind while filming The Good Old Days. I'm such an innocent, just seventeen, walking down the stairs from the Flys to the Green Room. On a window ledge at the bottom of the stairs sits Eartha Kitt dressed in Victorian green silk and feathers. She is looking up the staircase. She is looking up the staircase into my eyes. Directly into my eyes. Eartha Kitt is looking directly into my eyes. The Universe has come to a sudden stop because Eartha Kitt is looking directly into my eyes and she won't stop. There are twenty-four steps to climb down and her eyes don't blink or waver. I have to make you understand the full shuddering impact of that moment in my life. I was raised a Catholic in the Fifties being sent to the nuns at age four followed by an eternity under the iron fist of the Irish Christian Brothers ('We will instil a fear of God in your child'.). There had been only boys at my school. No girls. And certainly no Eartha Kitt.

When I tell people my Eartha Kitt story, I always pause at this point so that they can say: "Go on. What happened next?" I then take up the story. Her eyes followed me all the way to the kettle across the Green Room. When I turned from pouring myself a cup, she was still staring directly into my eyes. Pause. "And then what?" Nothing. She was called on stage for her cue and I retreated back to the Flys.

"Not much of a story," say my listeners. Maybe not to them and maybe not to you but to me, as I type these words, I am transported effortlessly back 50+ years to share a passionate moment in time with the one and only Eartha Kitt. And I know for a fact that despite what she sang and how she was dressed on that occasion, she was no old-fashioned girl. Eartha Kitt, Catwoman, looked directly into my eyes and stayed there for the rest of my life. That, Simon Cowell, is Star Quality.

Another memorable sex-bomb who trod the boards at the Varieties was Barbara Windsor. I'd enjoyed her performances in everything from The Rag Trade onwards but nothing for me beats the award winning moment she walked out of her dressing room towards the toilet at the end of the corridor. Passing me she smiled the famous grin and said the immortal line: "'Ello, darlin'!" That would have been more than enough to make my day. The fact that she was stark naked made my decade. Yes, I was enjoying the theatrical life.

In my second month at the theatre I started writing for comics. Not comic books but comics as in comedians. Jimmy Cricket and Little & Large appeared in an edition of The Good Old Days and mentioned they were looking for scriptwriters. Standing in the wings, listening to their material, I thought it would be impossible to write anything much worse, and so I picked up a pen. I knocked up two scripts each, learned to type, and mailed them off to their agents. Amazingly all four scripts were accepted and I got a cheque for £25.00 each by return mail! That was a lot of comic books and records back then!! Bingo! I suddenly realized I could write stuff. School certainly hadn't helped me come to this belief. If anything it had done the opposite. But school was now months ago. I was waking up…
By this time, one of my current favourite TV series was Monty Python's Flying Circus. I was over the moon when I heard they were going to do a theatre tour for the first time and pitch up in Leeds at the Grand Theatre. Turned out it was a night off for the City Varieties so I made sure I was working backstage at the Grand that day. Before the show, I carried a cup of tea into John Cleese's dressing room. We started chatting about the City Varieties, which is a theatre he wanted to see. I raved on about my time there and just how special the place was. I suddenly realized that sitting to one side of the dressing room was Eric

Idle, dressed only in an old raincoat and flat cap. He didn't say a word but stared intently at me. John questioned me more about the history of the Varieties and I filled him in but I suddenly started stammering as the intensity of Idle's inspection grew ever more invasive. I turned and looked at him. He carried on staring. No smile, just the stare. Very odd. Very off-putting. And nothing like Eartha! Good show though.

I'm many pages into my life story and I can't believe I haven't mentioned how great I am yet. Yes, there's a reason Bob Dylan wrote the song Mighty Quinn. Spike Milligan, All Time King of Comedy, is the reason. In my head. Spike came to the theatre with his one-man show. During the afternoon, he wandered over to where I was sat backstage, drawing a cartoon strip. He looked at one of the pictures and started laughing. Yes, Spike Milligan was laughing at my cartoon! I'll repeat that. SPIKE MILLIGAN WAS LAUGHING AT MY CARTOON!! And it got better. He then said these very words: "That's funnier than anything I have ever written." Now let me be the first to say that it most certainly wasn't. BUT, I made Spike Milligan laugh! I'm cool, I am. So push off anyone who disagrees. The cartoon? It showed a dog super-hero, the Shocking Sockstick, wearing a tartan sock on his head and carrying a curved tree branch in one paw as he swung upside-down from a trapeze above Manhattan. The caption read: 'Meanwhile, on an old abandoned trapeze high over New York City…' Comedy Gold! I have been a complete arrogant bastard ever since that day. Thanks, Spike.

The City Varieties closed each summer from June through September. In my first season there I had joined NATKE, a union for backstage workers that promised to get you a job in a London theatre at any time. So during that first summer break I called in at the NATKE office in London. They gave me an address of a venue in Soho that needed a stagehand. It turned out to be Raymond's Revue Bar, an 'exclusive' strip joint. Now that was a very strange experience for this Catholic schoolboy. The girls were fun and funny backstage with a certain to-hell-with-it attitude about life. Standing in the wings, it was a little stomach-turning to see the look on the faces of the audience as the girls went about their work. Paul Raymond himself was often there, coat draped over shoulders, drink in hand. He was very likeable with a twinkle about both eyes. Nuts, but likeable. Rumour had it that he owned more of London than the Queen. And Soho was Soho. Seedy but with a warm communal feel. I found I couldn't go anywhere without someone hissing from a doorway, "Psst! Do you wanna score?" I didn't.

Back in Leeds, during the panto we had a delivery of 2,000 comic books. These back issues had been sent by DC Thomson the publisher to be handed out to selected audience members who were invited up on stage to sing with Simple Simon, the Kiddies Friend. Between shows one afternoon, I picked up an edition of Sparky. It had been a favourite of mine way back in the mists of childhood, seven years ago. I found I still loved it. Especially Hungry Horace. Horace had been around since the Thirties. A simple idea, Horace was Hungry. That was the whole basis for the strip ... and it worked. Lovable rather than greedy-guts. I enjoyed the comic so much that I started drawing and writing scripts for the established characters of the comic while hanging out backstage during the day. I gave myself a month to see if I could come up with something close enough to a professional look. At the end of that month, I bundled up 4 strips and sent them off to Dundee.

Three weeks went by and I just got on with my theatrical life. It was fun. It was a real escape from so-called reality. Actors create their own world where anything goes. I liked that. Every day was an adventure. To quote Gerry Anderson, anything could happen in the next half hour. You'd better stand by for action. One of the stagehands belonged to The Sealed Knot Society. He would travel the length of the country re-enacting battles from the Civil War. He had the look of a gay cavalier, without the gay bit. He taught me how to swordfight up in the theatre attic. All sorts of old props and scenery became our battleground as we clashed up and down staircases, our shadows flickering across the walls. It is a wonder I still have two eyes. Two old coots playing Cinderella's Ugly Sisters fell for my curly-headed charm. They would push me into a corner backstage and lift up their crinolines to show zero underwear as they offered me £5.00 to enter their dressing room during the show's interval. No thank you. I could get five times that for writing a script. More appealing by far was Robinson Crusoe. This role was played by Pippa Boulter the daughter of John Boulter, one of the leads in The Black & White Minstrel Show. She told me that she didn't know whether her Dad was black or white until she turned four years of age. Pippa had blue eyes and they got me, damn them. When she bounded on stage in her leopard skin costume, smacked her fishnet stockinged thigh and declared, "All the nice girls love a sailor", I could quite see why.

And then the letter arrived. Postmarked Dundee. I hadn't had any rejections yet so I was quite hopeful. Quite right too as it turned out because even though they rejected two of my strips, they accepted two others and suggested I pop in should I be passing Dundee. Geographically it is highly unlikely that anyone living in Leeds would pass by Dundee, but I made sure I was passing by within the week and made my first visit to the realm of DC Thomson & Co Ltd. That letter had me walking on air for several days afterwards. I can still remember just how good it made me feel. I was gonna be in the comics! Sparky, no less, with Hungry Horace.

DC Thomson – Lots of Fun, For Everywun!

I liked Dundee as soon as I stepped off the train. It's one of those places that has something about it. A heartbeat. And it was Scotland. What's not to like. I found my way to Courier Place and stood for a minute looking at the DC Thomson building. It's quite a Gothic pile. It made me smile to think of all the outright naughtiness that had flown out of those office windows since the 1920's, encouraging children to be children. And now I was here to carry on that noble tradition. Children everywhere, pick up your peashooters and catapults and get revoltin'!

It was a slight let-down inside the building because there wasn't really much sign of out and out wackiness. A lot of offices and a lot of suits and a lot of people called Mr this or Mr that. A little straight after the weird and wonderful backstage world. However, it was DC Thomson and there were comic books everywhere I looked. I was met by Mr Chisholm, the editor of Sparky, which was a comic similar in style to the more famous Beano and Dandy weeklies. It was full of stories about naughty boys, girls, animals, and policemen. A fun read.

I found out later that Mr Chisholm had been in at the birth of Dennis the Menace, even scrawling the first image on the back of a cigarette pack. He was nice and funny and one of the people in the building who I didn't have to strain to translate from the Scottish. He signed me up on the spot to produce weekly stories for Hungry Horace, L Cars, Peter Piper, and a new character I was to develop titled 'The Adventures of a House Brick', which was based on a house brick. I think there was a certain Sixties thinking behind that idea. Mr Chisholm took me round the building to introduce me to the editors of the other titles, which brought in an unholy amount of work by the end of the week because there were a lot of weekly comics being produced at that time. Beano, Dandy, Topper, Beezer, Buzz, Bunty, Judy, Hotspur, and more. I headed back to Leeds and theatre-land loaded down with comics and work. After a few months I made the decision to find a place in Dundee and attempt to work full time in comics and mags.

I figured, quite rightly, that it would help keep the work coming in if I became a face rather than an envelope arriving in the editorial offices each week. The work flooded in and I found little time for anything else in my rather grotty little bedsit. The turnaround was fast and it was exciting to find my work in a variety of Thomson's publications. Not wanting to put all my eggs in one comic basket, I started writing for women's magazines and the Sunday Post newspaper, taking photographs and interviewing celebrities along the way. I was pretty nervous on my first interview.

It was at BBC TV Centre in London with Lesley Judd a presenter on the children's TV magazine programme Blue Peter. Fumbling with my tape recorder to start the interview, I accidentally opened the back panel and 8 batteries fell out to roll in every direction across the Blue Peter office. Lesley got down on her hands and knees to retrieve the bloody things from under cupboards and desks as I found myself awash with sweat. What a nice girl, even if she did then proceed to chain smoke roll-ups through the whole interview. She finished the interview by insisting I go out and buy Bob Dylan's Blood on the Tracks that minute. Good advice.

Meanwhile, back at the office I was writing a zillion strips a week. For the first couple of years I was more than happy continuing the adventures of long running characters such as Beryl the Peril, Korky the Cat, Peter Piper, Tiny the World's Largest Dog, Mickey the Monkey, Danny's Tranny (magical transistor radio in case you were wondering), Fred the Flop, Ball Boy, Dennis the Menace, Bash Street Kids, Ginger, Nobby(!), The Four Marys, and more. But then I had the urge to start creating more of my own characters. I kicked off with The Tyme Twins in The Topper. Originally this was going to be Tim Tyme and his Dog Grimm who found Time-Hopping pogo sticks, which allowed them to have adventures through history. We were all set to go with this idea when the editor had a hiccup and told me that the readers would have a hard time suspending disbelief at a dog time traveller. He insisted that Grimm be changed to Tina, Tim's twin sister. Shame, cos a dog gave a little more edge to the tales. Even so, it was fun to drop my characters into historical situations. I'd always enjoyed the adventures of Jimmy and his Magic Patch who was a time traveling schoolboy in The Beano back in the Fifties. The Tyme Twins was a little bit sillier but still the same history. I could always look in a history book for inspiration with that strip. It was the first but by no means the last time traveling strip I would produce.

Rummaging through back issues in Thomson's morgue one lunch time, I came up with a bright idea. Over the years, the company had produced many characters whose adventures had magical or fantasy themes. My idea was to pull all of those characters together and put them in one comic. Thomson's had once run a comic weekly titled 'Magic', so that seemed the ideal name to use for my magical new periodical. I put a dummy issue together and took it to the bosses. They seemed interested. Six months later they still seemed interested. Then another six months went by where they didn't seem interested at all. Finally, as I pushed for a yes or no, I was told that the kids of today were not interested in tales of magic so we wouldn't be going with the proposal. Kids not interested in magic? This was news to me in these pre Harry Potter days. I felt this was cobblers to put it mildly. Uh-oh, this was the start of me recognizing that the management had little idea of what their audience would like. In typical if peculiar style, Thomson's went on to launch a new Magic comic but it was aimed at the nursery age group and full of rather wet characters.

Never mind, I was still having fun and putting a lot of work into the DC Thomson annuals of the period. Games, puzzles, stories, strips, the lot. But... something was happening. Here's a good example. I was writing a Dennis the Menace script for the Beano Christmas issue. I set the tale on Christmas Eve and had Dennis turning the house upside down in an attempt to find his presents for the next day. The editor called me in and explained that he didn't think this was a suitable idea. "We don't want to encourage our readers to be sneaky." I couldn't believe my ears at the time. I still can't believe it now all these years later. This was supposed to be Dennis THE MENACE!! And kids are naturally sneaky when it comes to tracking down their Christmas presents before the big day. Little did I know that this was just the start. Bit-by-bit these gloriously naughty characters were being brought in to toe the line. Dennis the Menace, Beryl the Peril and Minnie the Minx were being tamed. I thought it was ridiculous that they were no longer allowed to be as naughty as they had been back in the Fifties especially as the Seventies were ten times more naughty. It was round about this time that I heard the phrase "We have to be careful here" in reference to our strips not giving offense to the easily offended.

Dicky Howett and IPC

September 1978 came around with word of a convention being held down in London to mark the 101st anniversary of the birth of comic books in the UK. Sounded a good idea to me, so I booked a ticket. It was an interesting mix of people there, from Leo Baxendale (there to launch his Willy the Kid book) and Bill Ritchie, mainstays of old DC Thomson's to ancients such as Terry Wakefield from Film Fun days, and new guys Dave Gibbons and Jim Baikie. Even Western thriller author JT Edson turned up. And there, in one corner, was a man wearing a Supermum t-shirt. It was, who else, Dicky Howett. I knew his work because he had recently started the strip Supermum in Whoopee comic. That strip stood out a mile mainly because the other strips either looked as though they were from the 1930's or drawn by people attempting (and failing) to do a Leo Baxendale. Dicky's work was funny and highly energized. We got chatting. And then we chatted some more. We decided to see if we could come up with a few ideas as a team to rejuvenate what we felt was the rather saggy world of funny comics in the UK. Over the next few weeks we turned out a ton of material. None of which ever saw the light of day. Here are a few examples:

Fred's Family Tree – Fred was a boy with a family tree scroll from which would pop his ancestors from caveman to Victorian.
Kids' Army – Dad's Army but with kids set in WW2.
Olly & Stan, 'They'll Do Anything For Cash' – Two boys determined to make their fortune before leaving primary school.

Harvey's Banana – Sounds a bit dodgy but it was a simple tale about an alien who could only be seen by a boy named Harvey (shades of James Stewart). The alien was in the shape of a banana.

Cross Road – There was a popular soap at the time titled Crossroads. This was a tale about a road where all the inhabitants were permanently cross with each other.

Dicky and I were churning them out on top of the weekly work we already had. Thanks to him I had taken over the scripting on his Supermum character in Whoopee. And I got a ton more work after we went for a lunch with Bob Paynter, the Head of Humour at IPC. This was the main rival to DC Thomson's comic weeklies. Bob reminded me of Liberace in looks but his character was more Grim Reaper. His first words to me were: "Hello, Tim. You do realize humour comics will be dead in five years?" I didn't but I could understand why the longer I worked at IPC. They were stuck in a rut and needed a good kicking. But first I signed on the line and gave them more of the same because they were much better payers than DC Thomson. Bob set me to work on titles across the line and even gave me whole annuals to script. A lot of work. Buster, Whoopee, Whizzer & Chips, School Fun (what a crap title!), and a flurry of teen mags on which I produced photo-strips, pop interviews and features.

Bob told me that he didn't think Dicky and I fit well together as a team. I disagreed. Bob did take one new strip of ours. The Gold Rush was about two brothers who had to take part in a marathon race round the world to determine who would win an inheritance. This got more difficult to write each week as Bob would send the script back repeatedly for changes. I noticed at one point that the script had been changed so many times that it ended up just as it had been when I first presented it. Not a lot of fun that.

Marvel Comics and Adolf Hitler

So financially IPC was very handy but I felt like I was falling asleep with the type of strips they were accepting. And all the time, humour comic book sales were slipping. And then one day IPC were caught in a strike that went on for six weeks, stopping all my strip work overnight. I looked elsewhere and called Dez Skinn who was running the UK office of Marvel Comics at the time. I asked him if he would have any interest in a Quinn/Howett funny strip to slot between the super-hero strips. No. He didn't think it would work with their audience. I have to say I agreed with him on that point. However, a few weeks later I heard that Dez had left the company so I put in another call to the new Marvel UK Head, a chap called Paul Neary. He thought the idea of a Brit type funny amongst the super-hero strips would go down a treat and asked if we could deliver a suitable strip for a new war comic they were about to send to the printer.

"Can you get us something the day after tomorrow?"

Bang! We were in. The strip was I Was Adolf's Double and the comic weekly was Forces in Combat. The story was all about a little innocent Jewish gardener who just happened to have the same face as Adolf Hitler at the worst possible time in history to have Adolf's face, World War 2. Paul changed the name of our gardener from Winston S. Cohen to Winston S. Quail for fear of offending someone somewhere. That turned out to be the only change Paul ever made to our work. As he said, he knew nothing about funny strips so he left it to us. I felt that the audience reaction would be pretty negative to our funny style popping up in a Marvel mag but I was wrong. Letter flooded in asking for more. And more we gave them. At that time, Marvel was producing about six weekly titles and four monthlies in the UK.

We ended up with strips in each of them. The strips were on a variety of subjects. Ever wondered what happened to the radioactive spider that bit Peter Parker? It went on to bite Dingle Dog who became The Fairly Amazing Spider-Hound. In Bullpen Bedlam we took a look at day-to-day life in the editorial office at Marvel. The Concise History of the Galaxy was exactly that but without the concise bit. Hulk the Menace was simply Dennis meets the Hulk. A ten year-old Incredible Hulk lives with his parents in a semi somewhere in England. Instead of a peashooter in his back pocket he had an axe. Finally I could let Dennis get naughtier than ever before. The Fantastic 400 were the world's largest super-hero group. Earth 33 1/3 was our take on Marvel's super-heroes. Absurd. Ridiculous. Hey, you wander around in skin-tights and a cape and someone's going to laugh at some point. For all Batman's grumpiness, the world of super-heroes is pretty funny.

The relief of not having editorial changes on every strip was enormous. It made us want to do even more. We suggested a weekly funny comic for Marvel. They said, let's see a dummy issue. That dummy issue sits in front of me on my desk at this moment. It's a great comic. We brought in various comic book chums to illustrate the various stories I wrote. Geoff Campion, David Lloyd, Ron Tiner, Martin Baxendale, and, of course, Dicky Howett. It was a nice mix of funny and adventure strips. Sadly, it landed on the MD's desk at Marvel and stayed there while they lost money on an all-new girls' comic they published. After six months the decision was made to stick to reprint material on new titles. Disappointing, but we still had our weekly and monthly strips at Marvel so we couldn't complain too much. I can't say the same about things back at IPC. There was a strip called Toy Boy(!). Every week the main character had adventures via a new toy he would be playing with. In one script I had him playing with a toy Noah's Ark. This was returned with the line: 'We don't bring religion into our comics.' For God's sake! Dicky and I produced a strip with the nursery title Playhour in mind. It was called 'Little Lost Ragga', and was all about a little dog who got lost in the Wild West. It had humorous overtones simply because all life does. The editor of Playhour told me, "Not for us. We don't deal with humour in our comic." I've meant to get that depressing line up on a t-shirt ever since.

I was also turning in scripts for TV Comic at this point. This had been another favourite weekly of mine from childhood so it was fun to be on board with the strips Popeye and The Inspector (Peter Sellers character). I'd always loved Popeye and had a collection of his old strips from the Thirties. I started bringing back some of the glorious old supporting characters to the strip such as the Sea Hag and the Goon. This was a lovely strip to work on. Unfortunately, early in the Eighties, the comic came to an end after a 30-year life that had seen characters as diverse as Doctor Who, The Telegoons, Coco the Clown, The Avengers (Steed & Mrs Peel not Captain America & Co), Mighty Moth, and Fireball XL5 grace its pages. I remember a fab free gift it once gave away during my childhood. A pack of Popeye's spinach! Can't beat that.

To promote Supermum, our latest Marvel strips and, most importantly, us, I contacted Rosemary Gill, the editor/producer of a Saturday morning children's BBC TV show, Multi-Coloured Swap Shop. I suggested we come on the show to demonstrate how comic books are made. To my surprise they thought this was a good idea and invited us in one Saturday to watch an episode going out live. Cliff Richard was the main guest that week and yes, he is as dull as you've heard. When he walked in the room I had the urge to fall asleep. Zero personality. Amazing from someone who has quite a tale to tell being in the Pop World through such amazing times but no, dull as dishwater. I blame God. Cliff was born again in the early Sixties.

Anyway, even meeting us didn't put the producers off, so we were invited to make our own appearance on the show the following week. It was quite something to turn up at BBC TV Centre and head to the make-up room. They did a great job and took days off our age. The show went well, I think. Noel Edmonds, the host, was particularly good at putting us at ease.

Even the presence of Adric, Doctor Who's Worst Ever Companion, and Jan Leeming, the BBC's Worst Ever Newsreader, couldn't put a dampener on the buzz we got from broadcasting to the nation. I felt we were great, naturals. Best bit was when I got the tube back into central London from White City. As I walked up into Oxford Street, a guy did a double-take and said, "Hey, you were on TV this morning!" I'd arrived! It's just a shame then that Dicky videoed the show so we could watch it later. Oh dear. Me. Awful. I would still cringe today if I had to watch it even though I am several lifetimes on. Talk about a learning curve. Ick!

And so the weeks and months and years clicked by. Dicky and I suddenly realized that due to our weekly workload we had turned out a hell of a lot of strips for Marvel. We suggested collecting many of them together as a Summer Special type title to test the water for attempting to produce a new humour weekly. There was a new MD at Marvel UK by this time so why not hit him with an old idea. He agreed that if the collection sold well then we could look at doing a weekly. And so we set out on a promotional trail to ensure that the Great British public were aware that Channel Thirty Three and a Third The Children's Comic was hitting the stands. We were in local press, on local radio and tv news programmes. It really must have been a slow news year because we got ourselves on everything.

Consequently the comic sold very well for a one-off type publication. Wahoo! Looked as if we were going to get our weekly after all this time. But life's not like that, is it? We had a great response from everybody who picked up Channel. Everybody that is except one person. A Dad. An angry Dad. A very angry Dad. He was so angry he sent a copy of the comic to his local paper claiming it was disgusting and full of mass murder, glue sniffing, prostitution, and copulation. In our defence I have to say, this isn't true. The comic wasn't full of these subjects. We merely touched upon them in some of the stories. Kids didn't have a problem. Nor did all the rest of the parents in the land. The newspaper decided to build a story round this Dad's rage under the headline: Anger Over Comic Smut. Look, Mum, I'm in the papers! The newspaper said it had done the decent thing and passed the comic book on to the DPP (Department of Public Prosecutions). Instead of saying bollocks to this, Marvel decided to drop us from all their mags except Doctor Who Monthly. "Just until the heat dies down." It took six months for the DPP to report that they could find nothing wrong with the comic, and by then Marvel had moved on. Bugger! Bugger! Bugger!

In retrospect this wasn't such a bugger after all. It made me move on. Viz was my first call. They couldn't have cared less that I was under investigation by the police. In their eyes it was a positive bonus. And Viz was funny … back then. I also put in a call to the Daily Mirror's Strips Dept. As luck would have it, I called at just the right moment and was given the scripting duty on their long running strip 'Jane'. Created back in the thirties, the main character was a 'bright young thing' who just happened to lose her clothes twice a week during each adventure. Sounds a little odd now but I was very pleased to be taking over such a historic strip.

I also mailed out the dummy of the humour comic we had put together for Marvel to Terry Jones of Monty Python. I had heard him mention his love of old comic books in a radio interview. A few weeks later I heard back from Terry in a well thought out critique of the comic. He liked most of the pages though told me that his young daughter loved every page. He offered to send £500 to help with getting the comic up and running. Very kind but at that point I had little idea on how to raise the rest. Terry also gave me the contact details to meet up with his friend Gilbert Shelton, the underground artist of the Furry Freak Brothers. The meeting went ahead in a mews in Chelsea, and very enjoyable it was too but our styles were too far apart to make sense of a team-up via Gilbert's publishing company.

Jane

Feeling a little gloomy that I was back to square one in humour comics, I picked up a copy of the latest edition of The Beatles Book. This was a monthly publication I'd bought since August 1963. By the Eighties the price had risen dramatically and I remember making the decision that this would be the final issue I'd buy. Flicking through I found an advert from a woman in the US who asked if anyone in the UK would like to swap houses for the Summer. Seemed like a good idea to me, so I wrote to her. By coincidence her name was Jane. And she wrote back. And I wrote back to her. And then she wrote back to me. Soon it became obvious we weren't talking houses. And so we met three months later, at Heathrow at 7:00am. My first word to Jane was: "Hoi!" as she walked past me, not yet used to British-sized short-arse people. We saw the sights of Liverpool, York, Southport, Leeds and London in the two weeks she was over here. On the final day we knew this was it. Love. And so we made plans that I would sort out a few outstanding work projects here in the UK and then move over to join her in Indianapolis.

Before I left, I mailed out an idea Dicky and I had put together for a Birthday Book to Sid Jacobson at Star Comics, the Marvel junior imprint of the time. Sid had been brought over to Marvel from Harvey Comics to launch the line. We claimed our book was the perfect extra gift for aunts, uncles, parents and grandparents to buy for little Tommy and Tina on their birthdays. Sid wrote me a very nice letter back saying how much he liked the proposal and execution, and inviting me to drop by if I found myself in New York. And so it was that I found myself in New York one sweltering summer's day, on my way to Indiana. Lugging an overweight shoulder bag with all my worldly clothes, I staggered into the Marvel Comics office for the first time. What an exciting place to find myself on my first day in NYC! Sid was great too. While he couldn't get Marvel or Star to invest in our birthday book he suggested I try scripting some of the Star line of characters. Not a bad first day in the US.

USA – The Saturday Evening Post Magazine

And arriving in Indianapolis, things got better with each passing day. I flipped through the local Yellow Pages under Publishers and found to my surprise that The Saturday Evening Post Magazine was based in town. The Post had been created by Ben Franklin back in the 1720's, and some of the best writers and illustrators had worked on the magazine ever since. F Scott Fitzgerald and PG Woodhouse to name but two. I phoned the editorial office and rather oddly was put through to the publisher herself. I explained my work in comics and cartoons in the UK and said I hoped to sell cartoons to the Post. She suggested I come into the office. I asked when would be a good time and she barked: "Now!" Well, that was different to how things worked in the UK. In Britain you'd make an appointment for weeks ahead, and you wouldn't get in to see the publisher but rather be fobbed off on some lowly editor.

Arriving at Waterway Blvd., I was shown into the publisher's office. Her name was Cory SerVaas, a tiny woman who was wearing a doctor's lab coat complete with stethoscope hanging round her neck. I handed her my portfolio of ghastly cartoons. She flipped through quickly and handed it back saying, "I don't know anything about humour." I was soon to find out just how true that statement was. "Whereabouts in England are you from?" she asked. "Liverpool," I replied. Everything stopped. She stared at me with a look of wonder in her eyes. "Liverpool? You're from Liverpool?" I smiled and nodded in agreement. "How'd you like to start work on Monday?" she responded. I was taken aback. I'd only gone in to sell a cartoon.

"Doing what" I asked. She thought for a moment before declaring, "You can be our Humor Editor. You guys are supposed to be funny from Liverpool, aren't you?" I could hardly deny that fact. I wandered out to the car where Jane waited patiently. "Did you sell a cartoon?" she asked. "I've got a job!" I replied. "How much?" asked the American. I dashed back inside the office to find out. Amazing. In a single bound I had gone from The Beano to one of America's most sophisticated magazines. Great Scott! as they say in the comics. Was I nervous? You betcha. I mean, I'd never been a Humour Editor before. Turned out that nobody else had been either. This was a brand new position created on the spot.

The following Monday as I entered the Post's reception, Cory hurried over to me and told me to wait there. "I have to go and fire someone to make way for you." Welcome to USA business style. Half an hour passed when a disgruntled former employee walked from the editorial office, carrying a cardboard box full of folders, stationary and a framed photo of his family. "Are you the British guy?" he asked. I nodded. "Well good luck, bud. You'll need it." Not much of a welcoming committee. After he had departed to shoot himself, Cory returned and walked me down several corridors to my new office. Someone was already taking the old name off the door and putting up a nameplate with the legend 'TIM QUINN – HUMOR EDITOR'. I had arrived.

Hanging on the wall behind my desk was a huge portrait of Richard Nixon. It somehow seemed apt that of all the presidents, he was the one on my office wall. "First thing I want you to do," said Cory as I settled in my swivel chair, "is to put together a book about AIDS for children. Do not mention homosexuals. I know I can trust you because I've met your wife." With that she turned and walked out of the office. I swivelled and looked up at Tricky Dicky. The word huh? came to mind. I mean, HUH?!?

The office wall was paper thin. I could overhear someone in the next office having a phone conversation. "Yeah, apparently he's English. And now he's our Humor Editor. How can an Englishman know anything about American humor?" Bloody cheek, I thought. I'd watched Mr Ed and My Mother the Car. But AIDS? This was in the early days of the disease. Nobody knew much about it, and everybody walked in fear of the word. I didn't want to know about it. I did know it had nothing to do with humor or even humour. One thing I found out that first day was that the Post also ran 7 children's magazines. Several of them had been running for decades and were a big part of American life. Jack & Jill, Humpty Dumpty, Child Life, Children's Digest, Turtle, Children's Playmate, and Stork. None of them had any strips so I told each editor that I would create a new strip for their particular mag. I had started work on this by midday when Cory came back into my office and asked how the AIDS book was coming along. "Erm...I'm just turning ideas of best approach over in my head while working up strips for the kids' mags," I babbled. "Well, hurry up," she barked. "People are dying!" Off she went again leaving me more bewildered than before. Was I supposed to come up with a cure now?

It was an interesting building I found myself in. Norman Rockwell originals lined the corridor walls and there was a display case of Benjamin Franklin's knick-knacks outside my office door. One thing became clear as I met more of my fellow editors. Everybody walked in fear of the boss. On my second day in the job I saw a grown man hide behind his office door when Cory came storming down the corridor. She seemed to be angry quite a lot. But not with me. After many hours of staring at a blank wall I'd hit upon a way to get the AIDS book up and running. My plan was to ask celebrities to mail in … anything. A poem, a drawing, a photo, a short story, absolutely anything; it didn't even have to have anything to do with AIDS.

I would place each celebrity's work on a page in the book and write a simple fact about the disease underneath it. My aim was to attempt to get rid of the stigma that was attached to the very word AIDS by showing that names in the public eye were supportive of sufferers. At this point in time the only celebrity who had his name linked with AIDS was Rock Hudson, and that was because he had the disease rather than that he was supporting people who had it. Of course, I didn't know if anyone would actually want their name attached to the disease. Regardless, I mailed off letters to the few celebrity names whose addresses I could track down. Three days later, my office phone rang. "Is that Tim Quinn?" asked a very recognizable voice.

"This is Yoko Ono. I'd like to help with your AIDS project." I was in business. I put in a call to the editor of the Los Angeles Times. Thanks to Yoko we got a front page story putting the word out that I was seeking celebs to help with the book. Over the next two months I was inundated with material from the biggest names of the period. Jane Fonda, the cast of Cheers, Gene Wilder, Charlton Heston, Joan Baez, Elton John, Hugh Hefner, the Pope, Dan Aykroyd, Mort Walker, Gary Trudeau, Phyllis Diller, to name but a few. Yes, THE Pope! Actually he sent a letter on Vatican stationary that ran along the lines of, 'I wish you well with your AIDS book, unfortunately I cannot contribute myself.' Ha-hah! thought I. You just have. So I got out my White Out and very carefully got rid of the 'unfortunately' line. That would do nicely as a greeting. But where to put the Pope's page in the book? I decided to put him face-to-face with Hugh Hefner's contribution, which was a cartoon drawing of himself. Talk about both ends of the sexual spectrum.

And then I got a very nice letter from Stan Lee at Marvel Comics. He wanted to contribute to the book using his Spider-Man character and also writing a piece of poetry calling for acceptance for people who had the disease. Thanks, Stan. During one of many phone conversations it turned out that Stan was a big fan of the 'Jane' comic strip I was still writing for the Daily Mirror back in the UK. Holy cow! Stan knew my stuff!! Now he was on board I headed over to DC to enlist Superman and Batman to the AIDS book. The company signed on as soon as they heard that Stan had contributed. So did Archie Comics. The book was turning into an extraordinary piece of work. Rolling Stone magazine rang to do an interview about the project. By now I saw the worth of the book. The timing was perfect and I do believe it helped in a tiny way to shatter the stupid stigma attached to the word AIDS. And it helped me to leap out of the comic book box I had created round myself.

Even so, this was a strange new world I was working in. One day I was called into a Very Important Meeting with the heads

49

of Kelloggs. They had a dilemma. Kids weren't eating All Bran. Cory thought as a person of humour I might be able to come up with fun reasons to get the children of America to put aside their marshmallow and chocolate morning cereals in favour of eating tree bark. She must be joking. Of course, she wasn't. Another time she asked me to come up with several cartoons to turn young people against taking snuff. I hadn't realized this was a problem since the Regency but Cory informed me that it was growing to epidemic proportions across the US with children burning holes in their heads through this particular substance abuse. I drew up a cartoon of a guy with a hole in his head and the caption: You need snuff like a hole in the head. Hilarious. I was cornering the Disease & Illness Cartoon Market.

You never knew who would be visiting the Post from day to day. Looking up from my work on one bright morning, I saw President Reagan walking by accompanied by a squad of security agents all in dark glasses. Later that same day, Fifties crooner Pat Boone knocked on my office door. He had heard that I had connections to Stan Lee at Marvel Comics. "I have a great idea for a Marvel Comic," he told me. "A team of handicapped super-heroes. They all have a handicap but they all also have a super-power. Do you think Stan would be interested in this?" I told him it sounded more suitable for a British comic magazine called Viz. While ignoring Pat Boone's wonderful creation I went time traveling again myself with a new slant on the travel side. My new creation was Tim Tyme for the Post's Children's Digest magazine. He had a new look and a new mode of transport. This time Tim soared through American history on a skateboard. The strip ran for fifteen years and is a favourite of mine to this day.

I know strange and I must say that the Post was a strange place to work. This was mainly down to our Boss Lady. I would arrive for work most mornings to find a stack of memos from her that had been delivered through the night. A typical memo ran: 'Tiny Tim, I want you to encourage our readers to donate their body parts after death. Can you start by drawing a cartoon showing a gangster type lurking in the shadows with a cigarette hanging from his lips like a flaccid penis. Go on to show how

50

smoking can hurt the organs so that they are useless for redistribution after death.' Believe me, that was a typical memo. The Humor Editor had his work cut out for him. I enjoyed creating new strips for each of the Post's seven children's mags. But even here Cory insisted that there would be health related topics on at least 18 pages of a 48-page publication. She wanted my strips to also feature healthy issues. I got round this with one strip by collaborating with Dicky Howett on an all-new version of The Fantastic 400. This time round they were called The Fitness 400. Happily, Cory only read the title and was appeased that I was following her direction. In fact the strips were as batty as any we'd done for Marvel.

It all began in Liverpool.
Great Grandparents back in 1875,
without whom

1956 on a grassy bank in my garden in Liverpool I find a magical comic book for the first time in my life. "Jack and the Beanstalk is the greatest story ever told." Stan Lee.

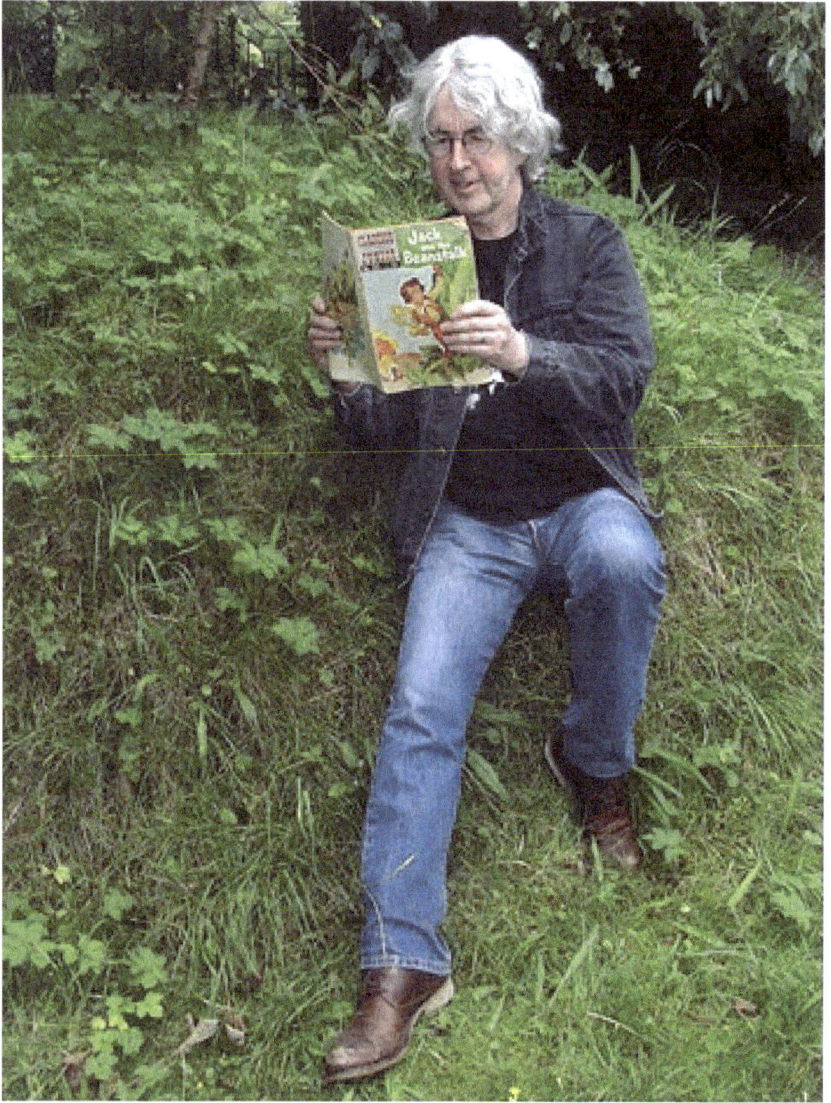

Same boy, same comic book, same grassy bank, different year.

Early work

Snowman 1959

Daleks versus Thunderbirds 1965

Early comic book sold at school 1964 featuring Wat Why,
a dog

St Mary's College for boys 1966 Front row 3rd from right. The
Sixties were banned from Swinging at this school.

Liverpool 1966 as seen by me from my
classroom window.

What to do on leaving school at age sixteen? I could be a priest
or work in a bank or....
First day at Blackpool Tower Circus.

Quinn & Howett regenerations

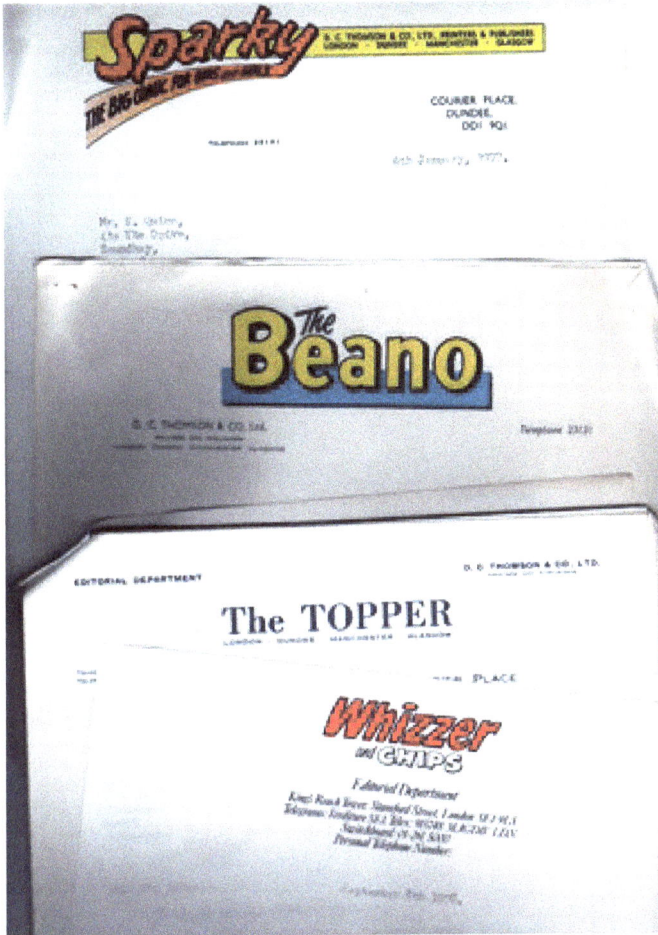

Tim Quinn
Head of Special Projects

New York London

Circus Boy and Indiana Girl
Jane & Tim

Humor Editor flies the flag in Indiana

Flyman at Leeds City Varieties Music Hall

MARVEL PRODUCTIONS LTD.
6007 SEPULVEDA BLVD.
VAN NUYS, CALIFORNIA 91413
(818) 988-8300 • TELEX #182325

STAN LEE

1/18/88

Mr. Tim Quinn
Humour Editor
The Saturday Evening Post
1100 Waterway Blvd.
Indianapolis
Indiana 46202

Dear Tim,

Thanks for your letter of 1/5 clarifying what you're looking for
in regards to the book you're doing for children relative to the
AIDS situation. (Wow! Talk about convoluted sentences!)

I was really stuck for an idea as to what to write, since I can't
think of too many humorous things to say about AIDS. Finally, I
resorted to a device I've often used when I had to write a column
for our comics-- I'd put my little message in the form of a poem.
I thought perhaps a simple verse that had some bearing on the
problem might do the trick for you now. And, after you read the
attached bit of poesy, you'll see why I'm known as a comicstrip
writer rather than poet laureate!

Anyway, I hope it'll serve the purpose. I'm also accompanying it
with a bit of artwork which you're free to use or not depending
on how it strikes you.

I trust this will prove satisfactory to you. If not, there's
time enough for you to let me know and perhaps I can come up with
something else.

Wishing you much luck with your project...

                                          Cordially,

                                          Stan

P.S. Be sure to send me a copy of the book when it's published,
or I'll send The Hulk after ya!

A NEW WORLD COMPANY

Letter from Stan Lee

62

Tim Quinn is pictured with comic superhero Spider-Man.

in-house editor and edited.

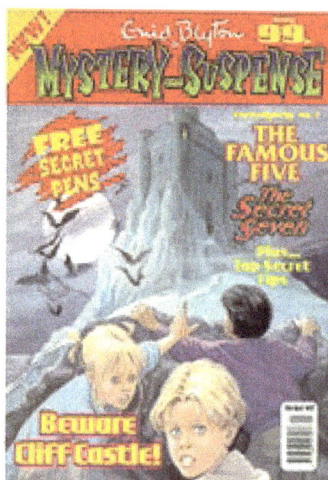

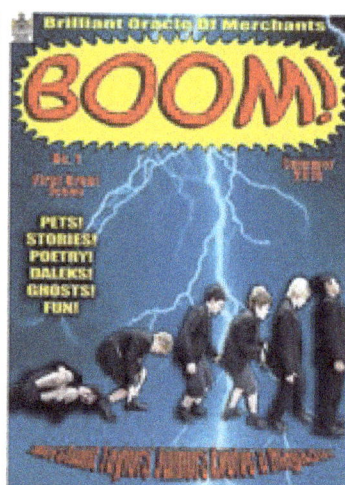

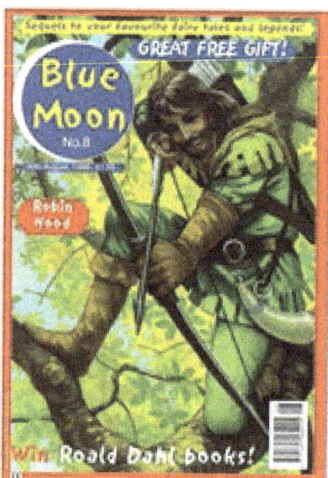

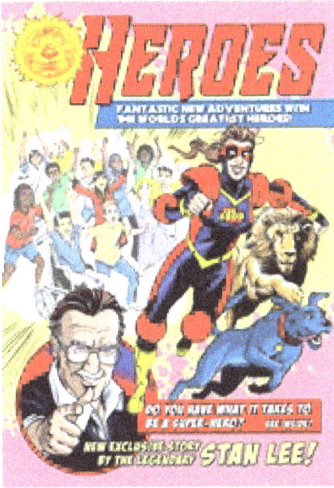

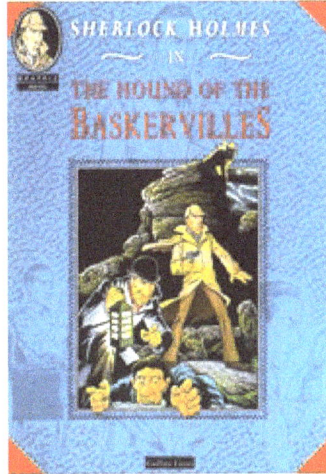

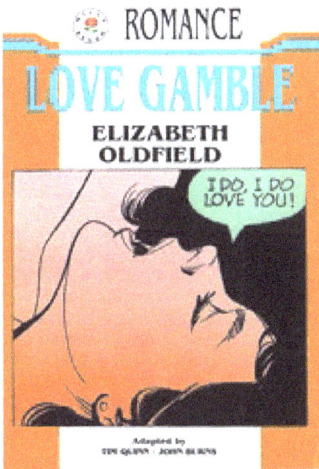

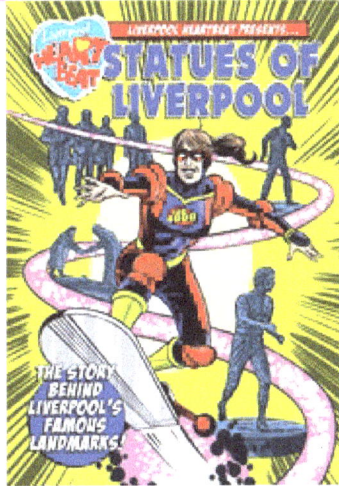

Quinn & Howett and Doctor Who.

Just Google 'Tim Quinn and Katy Manning' for a Youtube
interview on all things Doctor Who

Marvel editors, writers and illustrators play dress-up with
Mighty Quinn as Dr. Strange

The Brothers Quinn and friend.

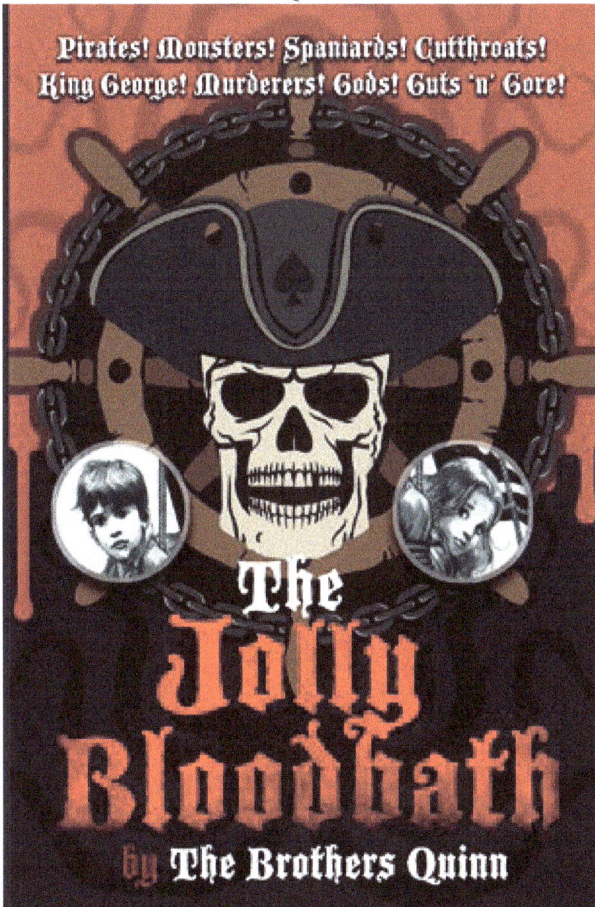

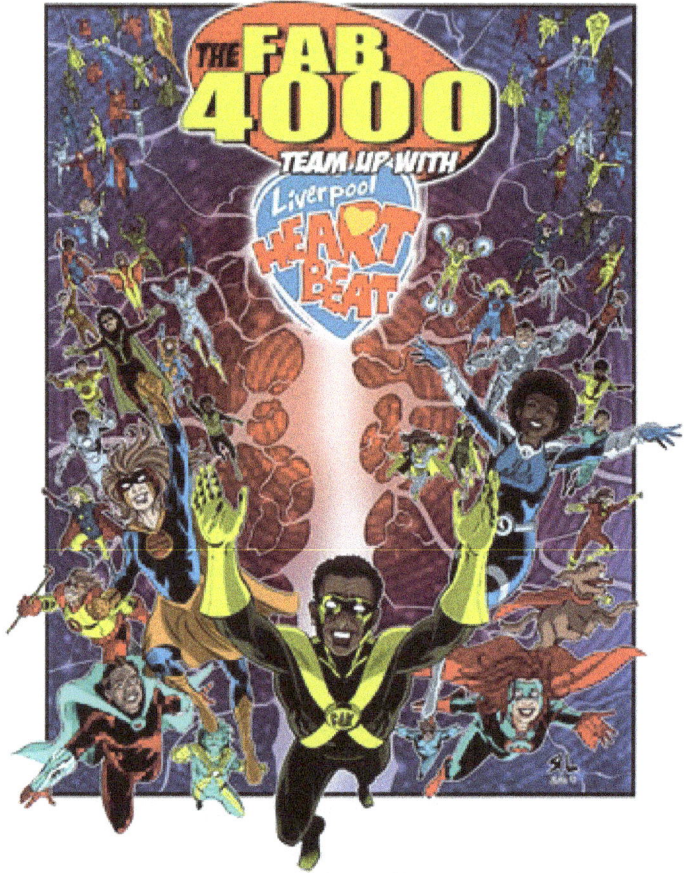

The Fab 4000, the world's largest super-hero team.
No knives, no guns, no weapons! Real heroes!

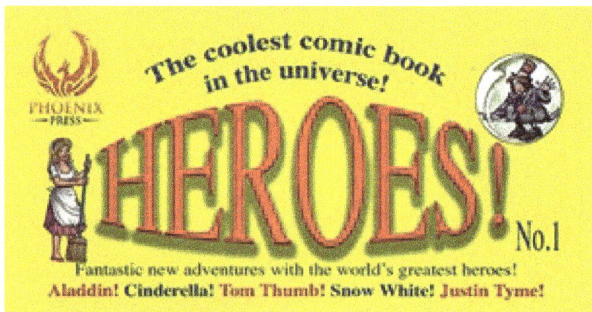

National Periodicals - DC Comics

Ever since Dicky and my aborted Beano style comic for Marvel UK, I'd been sending the dummy round to the odd publisher but always with zero luck. Chatting on the phone with Paul Levitz at Superman's DC Comics one day re the AIDS project, I asked if DC had any interest in humour comics. He told me that it was something they kicked around in editorial meetings every so often but that they hadn't come up with a suitable project yet. He suggested I meet up with one of his editors next time I was in New York. And so the following week I found myself sitting next to a dummy of Clark Kent in the DC reception. Mike Gold was the editor and we had a very pleasant afternoon and evening talking all things humour. The question was asked: Would a Beano style comic work in the US? The management at DC deliberated over this point for the next month before coming to the conclusion that no, it wouldn't. Oh well, never mind. Put the kettle on.

And then, sitting in my office at the Post one afternoon, I get two quite separate calls from England. The first was from a journalist named Don Short. Don was one of the main reporters who covered the Beatles stories during their touring years. We had met somewhere, some time. He was now running a syndication agency supplying features to publishers around the world. Don told me that he was in talks with Guinness to produce a comic book spinoff to their World Records book. Would I be interested in editing such a publication? I assured him I might well be. Putting the phone down it immediately rang again. This time it was John Brown, the publisher of Viz. I'd met John years before when he was running Pete Townshend's publishing company, Eel Pie Publishing. John told me that he was looking at the possibility of creating a junior Viz style comic. Would I be interested in putting a dummy together? Yes. What a day! Both very exciting projects and each with a hugely successful company behind it. What could possibly go wrong? Ha! This is the publishing world.

Actually, nothing went wrong. For ages. There were pages created and sent and meetings held. And weeks turned into months turned into years. And then, just as we were about to go with Guinness, new management stepped in and all present projects were canned. Meanwhile, over at Viz, goodness knows how many Viz ripoffs were now hitting the newsstands each month. A lot. All missing that one vital ingredient that made Viz work. They weren't funny. John Brown decided that the market was too cluttered to produce yet another Viz style comic although he did want to buy the latest version of The Fantastic 400 off me. I decided to hold onto it. I'm still holding onto it today. Ho-hum.

While working at the Post I was also creating strips for any number of magazines back in the UK. It was a time when editors still recognized that a regular strip would help add personality to their publication. It was easy enough to fashion strips after the general theme of each mag. Casting my net further I made contact with Mills & Boon, the romance publishers. I suggested they might bring in a teen audience if their books were adapted to the growing graphic novel format. They bought this premise and sent me 10 books to choose the first adaptation from. I read one and then the next and the next and the next before realizing they were all much the same so threw them all in the air and caught the winner. Somehow word of this venture got out and I was contacted by the editor of the Sun newspaper who told me he wanted to sex up his paper with a strip based on a Mills & Boon book. Obviously he had never read any of their books. Together with master illustrator John M. Burns I got to work on the adaptations. Fun in a can't-believe-I'm-doing-this kind of way. Despite a big launch with a full page of the strip, it soon became obvious that sexy wasn't exactly a staple of Mills & Boon storylines. Three weeks in I got a call from Editor Kelvin at the Sun. He came right to the point. "When's the sex start?" I explained that M&B were more into Romance. He made a noise down the phone line that went something like "Pfffff!" And that was it. The strip was dropped in mid story the very next day. Shame cos it was very well paid as newspaper strips were in those days. Over at the Daily Mirror I had come up with the idea of introducing real life characters into the Garth strip. The current story featured rock legend Tina Turner as Garth's girlfriend. Tina gave me a great quote about her appearance in the strip. "This is better than getting the cover of Vogue." The Mirror splashed the quote over a 2-page spread at the start of that particular story.

Sherlock Holmes

A project of sheer joy at this time was working with Gyles Brandreth to turn out 3 comic book adaptations of Sherlock Holmes stories. How to describe Gyles? He is Gyles Brandreth and I love him dearly. He should be running Great Britain, even his initials fit. Anyway, I'd met him years earlier and it turned out we both had a love of all things Conan Doyle. Amongst a thousand other jobs, he was running an editorial packaging company called Complete Editions. He sold the idea of Holmes in comic strip format to Collins Books and we were away. We chose the stories 'The Hound of the Baskervilles', 'The Speckled Band', and 'The Blue Carbuncle'. I wanted to give the books a Tintin feel so chose the American illustrator George Sears to supply the artwork. I traveled round Britain to promote them on the week leading up to their launch. I found that local radio and TV news was only interested in stories that were grounded locally. To get over this I claimed in each area that the background illustrations were based on buildings in each town. Nonsense, of course, but it got me on each programme.

Marvel Comics again

While in London for a meeting with the Strips Dept at the Daily Mirror I had heard that Marvel UK was expanding in a big way. They were churning out a ton of brand new work to launch over in the US, and they were looking for editorial staff. Interesting. Back at the Post in Indianapolis I was called into the publisher's office one day soon after this UK trip. Cory told me that she had received a letter of complaint about one of the stories I'd written for Jack & Jill magazine. She handed me the letter. It was postmarked Alabama. Alarm bells immediately. It was from the mother of a regular reader of Jack & Jill and began in the time honoured way of letters of complaint with the words: "Dear Editor, I was disgusted…" She was disgusted to find that my story featured an elf living in a tree house with a robin. Or, as the mother put it, 'co-habiting'. I laughed out loud as I read the letter and asked if I should file it under wastepaper basket. But Cory was not amused. "We must take this seriously. This is one of our subscribers. We cannot afford to upset them." ARGH! I hate that kind of thinking. It ensures that you create magazines and comic books aimed at the tiny percent who write letters of complaint rather than the tens of thousands who don't. Madness. Publishing today. I went back to my office, passing evangelist Lester Sumrall in the corridor. The very sight of him made my mind up and put in a call to Marvel. I started working for them the following month as an editor.

Always make a good impression on your first day. My plan was to be first in as soon as the doors were opened. Unfortunately I misjudged trains at the slightly busy Clapham

Junction and found myself on a non-stop to Kent rather than the four-minute trip to Waterloo. I wasn't the first in when I finally turned up at Arundel House at 10:45 am. Thankfully, Marvel UK's time code was a little different to the Saturday Evening Post Magazine where I'd actually had to punch the clock each day. At Marvel you came in and just got the job done. Time went out the window. The office was in a fab location on the bank of the River Thames at Temple, a part of the city of London that had been established by the Knights Templar back in the Crusades. The chimney pots atop Arundel House dated from Tudor times. I would find myself up amongst them on many an occasion.

First up though was Spider-Man's 30th Anniversary. As I was editing the Spidey comic I thought it was the perfect time to bring in some promotion. However, the media did not agree. At that moment in time they couldn't have cared less whether Spider-Man was 30 or 130. To them it simply wasn't a news story. I would have to think again. In the meantime I found that the location of the London office was very handy for lunch with the Strips Dept of the Daily Mirror. Over one such lunch with John M. Burns, strips editor John Allard, and Perishers creator Maurice Dodd, I mentioned my new 'Marvelous' job. "Those idiots," said John A. "We've been wanting to run the Spider-Man daily strip for the last six months but their licensing department doesn't bother responding to our phone calls or letters." I thought there must surely be some mistake as Spidey in the Mirror would be a fantastic daily promotion for the company. I promised to look into it on my return from lunch. I found that I was right. There was some mistake. The mistake was called Marvel's Licensing Dept. They held office on the top floor of Arundel House. They had the carpets, view and curtains while we in editorial had the floorboards. "Oh yes," said their Glorious Leader who shall remain nameless so I can tell it like it was. "Leave it with us. We'll get back to them." They never did so the Daily Mirror remained Spiderless. Strike one of 3,567.

My wife Jane, strolling in Chelsea one day, discovered the Jane Asher Cake Shop. She went in and was surprised to be served by former Beatle girlfriend and actress Jane herself with a cuppa and cake. When I heard the tale that night it gave me an idea. Back at Marvel the next morning I phoned through and spoke to Jane asking if she would make a cake to celebrate Spider-Man's 30th anniversary. She thought it sounded fun and agreed at a cost of £185. She also agreed to me bringing Spider-Man himself around to the shop to collect it along with as many newspaper photographers as we could muster.

I got back in touch with all the nationals and found that now they were interested. Spidey meets Jane Asher with a cake was a news story and a photo op. I was also able to sell the idea to TV and radio programmes. I ended up with seven TV spots over a 2-day period. Not a bad promotion for an outgoing of £185. And that would have been the total cost but for the fact that our Licensing Dept got to hear of my plans. They weren't happy.

"This doesn't really fit in with our plans," I was told. "What plans?" I asked. "Who have you got to play Spider-Man?" they asked, changing the subject. "I have an actor friend who is fairly pumped up and has agreed to play the part for the two days," I said. "Is he American?" "No, he's Dutch." Sharp intake of breath. "Well that won't do. Spider-Man's American!" Sharper intake of breath from me this time. "I am aware of that. My actor friend is very good at accents." The Heads of Licensing shook in the negative. "Leave it with us," they said ominously. That was the day that the Marvel Editorial Dept started calling the Licensing Dept the *Fucking* Licensing Dept.

The following day all hell broke loose. I was summoned to a meeting of the heads of the Editorial and Licensing Depts. I was informed that New York wasn't happy at all with what I'd done. They were so unhappy that they were sending over two of their top guys from management the very next day to try to "clean up this mess". I had to ask: "What mess?" I was told that promotions of any kind must be handled carefully and only at certain times each year. "But we have comics out every week of each year," I protested. "We need to promote them all the time." Shaking of heads. "Your promotions are not in line with the general directive," declared the Licensing Head, showing her Dalek roots.

Sure enough the two Top Guys arrived a day later. We kicked off with what was the most pointless meeting of my life. A five-hour meeting talking about a cake. They were concerned that Jane's cake might not meet management requirements for images of Spider-Man. "It's a cake," I protested. "Doesn't matter if it's a John Deer tractor. If it's in the image of Spider-Man it must meet our standards. Where are Jane's plans for the cake?" Now I knew for a fact that Jane wouldn't draw detailed plans in her cookery. She would just make the bloody cake. I also knew I was not going to ask her to draw plans for such a cake. And so I said: "Okay, I'll go and phone her and get her to taxi round the plans."

Once out of the room I hurried down to the Marvel basement where we kept our artists. I explained my predicament. They were happy to help. Twenty minutes later I had my detailed plans for the Spidey cake. I took them back into the meeting room. The Licensing mugs poured over them, humming and harring. "We will still need to see the cake before we let it go on television," one of them declared. Purely as a joke I then said, "Maybe we should get Jane to make a second stand-by cake in case the first one doesn't come up to requirements?" Instead of telling me to fuck off like I expected, the knobs actually said: "Great idea! Get her on it now." Out of the room and on the phone to Jane. I explain the situation. She laughs loud and long. "I've worked for such people before," she assures me. "So can you make a second cake for us and please do me a favour and charge the earth because all thoughts of saving the company money have now gone out of the window with them shipping folk over from New York." Second cake in the oven.

On the next day these knobs auditioned my actor friend to play Spider-Man. We had a rather moth-eaten costume that looked like it had been stuck in a drawer for years. But the costume is such a great design that it immediately comes to life with the right body type inside it. My mate bounded into the office in front of the New Yorkers and our own UK Marketing Dept. Several Spidey-like leaps and dives around the room ended at the window, which was thrown up and, in a single bound, my friend dramatically jumped outside. Keeping in mind that we were on the second floor and this was Bill rather than Peter Parker, it was one hell of an audition. He was even wisecracking as he clung to the ledge outside. After Bill had left, the judgement came down. They thought he had filled the costume adequately but that his accent let him down (rubbish! He had a more believable accent than the New Yorkers), and so we would use Bill merely for the newspaper photos but bring a real live American actor over for the TV spots. Ker-Ching! This cheapo-cheapo promotion was now ringing up big bucks.

The day arrived when the cakes were finished. I accompanied the combined Marketing Departments in a taxi over to Jane Asher's Cake Shop in Chelsea. She had placed both cakes on pedestals on a table top. Jane and I shared a look of amusement as the Marketing folk set off on an exploratory tour round the table, ducking and diving as they went to get the best view of both cakes. Standing back, their leader nodded in satisfaction although he couldn't resist pointing out: "You've missed a bit of colouring on the bottom edge of the second cake." Jane assured him that would be dealt with before the press arrival the following morning.

And they turned up in their hoards. It was quite a sight seeing each photographer from each national attempting to pose our Spider-Man and Jane Asher + cake in a new and fun way. "Look this way! Look that way! Look the other way! Look up! Look down!" My favourite shot was the one where it looks as if Jane is helping Spidey climb up a drainpipe, all the while clutching one of the huge cakes. Thank God for spider-powers! Jane's two young sons had come along to meet Spider-Man and I presented them with a big load of Marvel goodies. Their Dad, the satirical political cartoonist Gerald Scarfe, was also with them. I took the opportunity to ask him if he would do a cover for my Spider-Man comic. As his sons were listening, he could hardly say no. What a coup! What a day! Time to change Spider-Men for the New York version and jump in a cab to head to Sky TV News. On the way I noticed that this Spidey had rolled up his mask and was busy rolling a huge joint. I could picture the headlines: SPIDER-MAN AND EDITOR CAUGHT IN DRUGS HAUL! Having always been a Just Say No kind of guy, I grabbed his stash and lobbed it out the window as we sped through Kentish Town. This made for a pretty pissed Spidey for the rest of the day.

In the Sky TV News studio we were interviewed by Kay Burley who seemed as pissed as Spider-Man at having to do a comics related story. "What do you think of other super characters such as Superman and Batman?" she asked us. Without a pause, Spider-Man leapt up on her desk and replied: "You've got to wonder about a guy in a cape." Nice Spider-like answer.

The next morning found US Spidey and me + a cake on our laps on a plane from London to Liverpool for an appearance on ITV's 'This Morning' magazine programme hosted by Richard & Judy. New York had sent us special solid silver Spidey badges to present to R & J. We were accompanied on the flight by Ulrika Jonson who was hosting ITV's 'Gladiators' show at the time. Spidey took a liking to Ulrika on first sight. "Man, will you look at that rack!" he declared. By the time we were in the studio Green Room, I found him down on one knee in front of the lovely Ulrika, presenting her with one of the silver Spideys. She wore it on the show. I kept the other one for my wife as both Spider-Man and I took an instant dislike to Richard and Judy.

By the end of this second day we were booked in to deliver both cakes to London's Children's Hospital. Spider-Man was to make an appearance in the Isolation Ward, waving at the patients through a glass window as he held up the two cakes. Unfortunately he failed to see a child's plastic chair near the window and tripped head first in a very Ditko-like manner. His Spider-sense was operating in fine form though as he managed to catch both cakes before they hit the ground, and the sickly kiddies duly got their serving of Spidey sugar-rush.

Next day at the office I was told that having Gerald Scarfe do a cover for us wasn't on as it would not go down well with the fans. I explained that it would bring us new fans and also be quite a news story but there was no convincing. "Tell him he can do a feature page inside the comic but not the cover," suggested my MD. Yeah, right! And so we didn't get the Scarfe cover. It still irks all these years later.

The South Bank Show

Hitting the fifth decade anniversary of Marvel Comics I wrote a letter to Melvyn Bragg, producer of London Weekend Television's 'South Bank Show' documentary series suggesting the Marvel tale captured a part of American culture that deserved chronicling. To my surprise I was invited to a meeting directly across the Thames in LWT's tower block. Melvyn invited me to co-produce the episode along with his Senior Director Daniel Wiles. What an opportunity both for Marvel and for me! Yes, please. It was agreed that we would split the programme in half, filming part one in New York while part two would be shot in our London office showing how UK talent was breaking into the super-hero world. Fantastic promotion for Marvel as a whole. Who could possibly have a problem with that? Cue my office phone. It was the Licensing Dept from upstairs. "What's this we hear about the South Bank Show producing an episode about Marvel? We would never have agreed to this. The timing is all wrong. We would have chosen to do something like this two years from now." I counted ten extremely quickly. "Well do something like this two years from now as well. We will still be here and still need promotions. The editorial department is putting out material now which means we need to promote it now!" Amazing. Not one swear word left my gob, but there was a dictionary full of them cluttering up my brain.

We went ahead. A wonderful learning curve for me working alongside Daniel Wiles who became a friend for life. We laughed at the same things and same people. Arriving in New York we found a film crew setting up outside our hotel in Times

Square. As we were heading in, Arnold Swarzenegger was coming out to film a promotion for his latest movie. We were there for a week but determined to shoot all necessary footage over 3 or 4 days so we could have the rest of the time gadding about the city.

Arriving at Marvel early the following morning, our film crew set up establishing shots of the skyscraper base along with passing yellow cabs. Once inside I was warned by the Head of Marketing not to mention DC Comics at all during our interview with Stan Lee. "Under no circumstances mention Superman or Batman as we do not want to promote our rival. And I will stop the interview if you do not stick to this rule." Nice welcome. Stan arrives and tells us we can ask him anything as long as it relates to the last five minutes. "I can't remember a thing before that," he laughs. On our first question about how he got into the business, Stan details the creation of DC Comics and the birth of Superman and Batman "who we owe everything to." I see the Head of Marketing tense off camera but she knows better than to stop Stan the Man. One of those great interviews as Stan covered comic book ground from the Thirties through to the present.

Back in the UK I had a bright idea for the opening shot of the programme. We would go up on the rooftop of LWT and pan downriver from Waterloo Bridge up the Embankment to the Marvel UK office at Temple where we would have Spider-Man skittering around amongst the chimney pots as a voiceover announced that America's finest comic book company was now taking over Britain. It was a great clip that stands up today alongside Stan's interview. To promote the episode, the South Bank Show held a Comic Book Workshop on a boat on the Thames. This turned into a show I developed further to play in schools and art centres both in the UK and US. My brother Jason had joined Marvel as an editor by this time and he did the honours in the Spider-suit on this day.

Head of Special Projects

By this time I had become the Head of Special Projects at Marvel, which suited me as it meant nobody knew what I was working on at any given time. During one editorial meeting I made the suggestion that as Marvel had been a successful part of the Macy's Thanksgiving Day Parade for a number of years we could do a similar event in the UK. For example the Lord Mayor's Parade. The MD liked the idea and said, "Go do it." It wasn't long before I regretted making that suggestion.

The first thing you get after handing over your cash to the Lord Mayor's office is a 50-page Book of Rules For Attendance in the Parade. I must get round to reading it one day. I was too busy at the time designing the official Marvel float. Big as a double decker bus, because that's exactly what it was underneath all the explosive illustrations of Marvel's finest. I made sure there was a nice mix of Marvel US and Marvel UK creations. It looked good on paper and even better on the bus! I booked for ten super-hero costumes to be shipped over from our New York office. The idea was to hire American size actors to fill the suits on the day of the parade. However, the float went over budget leaving me with zero cash to go in search of actors. Only one thing to do…head round the Marvel UK offices and convince our editors, writers and illustrators to suit up. For the first time since my Blackpool Circus days I was back in costume, as Doctor Strange, Sorceror Supreme. He had the warmest cape and as the parade was in November, this was a wise move. It took some convincing to get my British short-arse band of heroes into costume. There was much rolling up of trouser legs and tucking in of tops on the American-sized suits. There was only one thing to do once in costume though and that was to take to the rooftop for a photoshoot. Posing exactly like the characters we'd seen a million times in the comics we looked pretty darn good if I say so myself. Wolverine in particular put the comic into our group photo.

The night before the parade I received a call from the New York office. "You won't get the costumes wet, will you? You do realize they come in at a total value of several thousand dollars?" Rain? In November in London? Hardly likely, I assured them. So you can imagine my surprise the next morning to wake at 5am to the sound of torrential rain. And it kept up through most of the day. It was also bloody cold. We met at base camp for the parade at 7:30am. My band was in good spirits regardless of the weather. The Lord Mayor's chamberlain came running over to me to say that the designated room we had for suiting up had been changed and that we would now have to change in a gentlemen's toilet. "No we won't!" I blew a gasket as the toilet he suggested was a pit we had already complained about. An argument ensued, which I won by simply shouting the loudest. Brute force from Doctor Strange. Once in costume we headed out to the float in the pouring rain, Captain America using his mighty shield as an umbrella. Standing shivering beside the float for a photo, we were jeered at by a group of passing soldiers who were on the float in front of ours. As if that wasn't bad enough, we were then laughed at by a passing Blue Peter presenter. I guess on ground level we did look a pretty weedy bunch.

It was a different scene by the time we took our places atop the float. We looked truly Marvelous (it had to be said). Off we trundled. 5 bloody hours we were on that float, waving down to the millions of people lining the route across London. It is something I will never forget. The rain, the cold and being cheered round London's landmarks. An image that comes to mind is of Spider-Man, halfway round the course, rolling his mask up in an attempt to get a bit of warmth from a crafty cigarette.

Finally it was over. One quick change and we carted the sodden costumes back to the editorial office where we turned the heat up to high and draped them around the room. As it was Saturday, we hoped they would be dry by Monday morning. And everything was dry by Monday morning. I shoved all costumes carefully back into the packing crate and had it collected for Return to Sender. We were featured strongly on TV coverage of the parade but it was a lot of work for one day's telly.

"Keep in mind that our audience of readers are fourteen year-old morons." So declared my immediate boss at Marvel UK. I hadn't been aware of this. I'd never had any desire to do anything for morons of any age. But this was his view and it could be argued if you look at the material we were putting out at this time that this could be the only explanation for the direction the books were taking. I sat in on one editorial meeting where the main thrust was trying to come up with more titles with the word 'Death' in them. I suggested 'Deaf Old Git'. The books we were putting into the US had an initial success but sales dropped drastically from issue 2 onwards. I guess the 14 year-old morons of America had better things to spend their money on. This was still a time when the word Marvel on a comic would guarantee readers picking up the first issue at least. But those readers weren't going to hang around if they didn't like what they found on opening each book.

Enid Blyton

At the next editorial meeting our MD asked for ideas outside the super-hero line. I suggested producing a weekly title adapting the work of Enid Blyton into the comic strip format. Blyton's books had sold well since the Twenties so Grandparents, parents and children themselves were a guaranteed audience. Various editors round the table objected.

"Blyton's racist!"

"She's sexist!"

"Enid Blyton's fascist!"

Luckily our MD shared all of these personality traits and told me to look into the idea. Blyton, of course, was none of these things, but our idiot PC world of the media had been taking snipes at her success for years. For me the important thing was that children loved her stories and were hooked by the end of the first paragraph.

I set up a meeting with Enid's elder daughter, Gillian Baverstock. Gillian had successfully run the Enid Blyton Company since her mother's death years before. She was everything you would want the head of such a company to be. We hit it off right away and set about choosing the best stories to make up a weekly comic. I wanted to use Marvel style artists to bring Blyton's stories to exciting life. Back at the office I told Sal Buscema, a US illustrator over on his holidays, about the comic. He hadn't heard of Enid Blyton so I quickly gave him a rundown of one of her books, 'The Wishing Chair'. Every so often the Wishing Chair would grow wings on each leg and whisk two children and their pixie friend off for adventure after adventure in places such as the Land of Giants, the Land of Fairy Tales, or the Land of Stupids. As I spoke he picked up a pencil and produced a wonderful sketch of two kids holding on for dear life as a winged chair soared over the rooftops of a town. Yes, this was going to work!

From the sublime to the ridiculous. I got a call from Paul Raymond no less. He knew I was writing the 'Jane' strip in the Daily Mirror and thought it would be a good idea to have a double-page naughty-but-nice strip in his monthly publication 'Club International'. I thought so too when he told me the fee. I nipped down into the Marvel basement and asked the assembled artists if anyone fancied illustrating such a strip. All hands went up and that's pretty much how the strip was done from thereon. I would hand in the script down in the basement and everybody would pitch in to the glorious adventures of SEXBOMB, a Marvel type heroine whose superpower was that she could give anyone an instant orgasm thereby stopping them in their tracks. Subtle or what? We just had to make sure the strip was out of sight whenever we allowed any children in to tour the Marvel offices. The strip ran for about a year and surely to goodness should be at the top of any Marvel UK fan's Collect List!

Beatles, Fairy Tales and Idjuts

Meanwhile back in the US I was also working on the Marvel Music Line of books. This was the very simple idea of getting top musicians to work with our illustrators and writers to create something a little different. Alice Cooper was first up working alongside Neil Gaiman. Arriving at Marvel one day Alice's first words to me were, "Hey, man, where's the john?" I treasure those words as much as the book and album he produced for Marvel. Different, quirky, wonderful. The Rolling Stones, Bernie Taupin and Elton John and the Beatles were next. I contacted Derek Taylor, publicist at the Beatles Apple company, and arranged a meeting with Neil Aspinall, the Fabs' manager of sorts. Neil had been with them from the start and knew them through and through. He asked me who was going to dialogue this retelling of the Beatles story. I told him that I was putting myself up for that position. "But how will you have them talking?" This didn't faze me and I answered, "Well I know how they talk. I've seen A Hard Day's Night and Help many times." Neil shook his head. "That's not how they talk." Oh! I admitted defeat. "In that case we need someone on the inside to write the book," I said, turning to Derek. "How about it?" Derek was happy to work for Marvel on creating the comic book tale of the Beatles as he had never written a strip before. "I'll guide you," I promised. And so for the whole of that summer Derek and I would meet over lunch every Friday to discuss the project. The lunch would last through dinner time and I swear we always spent a good five minutes talking about the Beatles project. The rest of the time was spent listening to Derek's amazing tales of his life in music. That suited me.

Christmas fell at the end of this particular year, just like most years. I had the bright idea of releasing a Father Christmas comic in mid November to get children in the yuletide spirit. The book would feature a strip story about FC along with puzzles and festive features. Scripts were written and all was go until I was called into an editorial meeting where our Head of Marketing declared: "We shouldn't risk launching a comic with a new character at this time." I explained that this was hardly a new character but there was no moving the thick get. Voices were raised and doors were slammed but the book remained canned.

Still in Fairy Tale mode, I put together the dummy first issue of 'Happily Every After?', a series of sequels to the world's most famous fairy tales. It had never seemed right to me that such wonderful characters as Snow White, Jack of the Beanstalk, Cinderella, Aladdin, Sleeping Beauty, etc., had only ever had one adventure and then settled for living happily ever after. This comic book would take up the tale two weeks after the end of their original adventures. Each tale in the comic would feature a completely different art style. I wanted to reclaim these characters from the Disney look and bring them back to their European roots. As the pages came in, the project looked better with each day.

And then Marvel Comics went bankrupt.

Yes, the top selling comic book company in the world went bankrupt.

Suddenly there was no money anywhere. Every upcoming project was canned. People were fired or 'let go'. So many people were let go one Black Friday that by the time Monday came around management realized we no longer had enough people in house to do the work we were still producing, so a phone call was made to bring back somebody who had been fired

3 days earlier. Definition of management: Goldbrickin' meatheads.

So there I was one fine day, sitting at my desk, packing up artwork to send back to one of our artists. In came the MD. He noticed I was using a hard-backed envelope. "Do you know how much those things cost?" he asked. "And they add to the cost of the postage too. Use a normal envelope." We were watching costs by this time, you see. The Accounts Manager had overheard this conversation. She came over to me and revealed that our glorious heffalump of a boss had just handed her a £500 receipt for his lunch at the Savoy that day. This was pretty common practice as it turned out. Teaming up with another member of staff we realized that the company would soon go belly-up under this guy's management, not just because of his lunches but also his general lack of savvy about the business. We decided there and then to put together a dossier on the bloater to send over to New York to get them to either kick his ass into gear or out of the company. Over a period of six months the dossier became almost as fat as the man it was about. We shipped it Special D. Next thing we knew, a delegation of Marvel Management arrived at the offices in London early one morning. By midday we had a brand new MD. There was a good feeling at the Edgar Wallace pub that night. We would survive.

Ha!

Radio Ga-Ga

…And then I got a call from BBC Radio 1FM. I had completely forgotten that 12 months previously I had sent their programme controller the suggestion of creating a daily cliffhanger drama series featuring Spider-Man and assorted Marvel characters. He now invited me in to talk the project through. A successful meeting led to me being introduced to Dirk Maggs, producer extraordinary. We got on from the get go and had soon knocked up the overall storyline for a 50-episode serial of 5 minute segments. Our aim was to recapture the sheer joy of Stan Lee's Marvel Universe stories from the Sixties. Dirk pulled in a masterly group of actors, and one of the highlights of my career was watching him conduct them like an orchestra in the studio.

The end result was the most visual comic book I have ever worked on despite there being no illustrations created. The music helped. I'd written to Brian May of Queen to see if he had any interest in composing a Spider-Man theme. To my surprise, he did. I turned up for a meeting at his office and suddenly caught sight of myself in the reflection of the glass door as I entered the building. I was wearing jeans, a white shirt and black waistcoat. This was a look I'd worn for years but suddenly had the awful realization that with the mop-top of curly hair I appeared to be a tribute act to Brian. Meeting me in the foyer, Brian did a double-take. "Have we met before?" "Maybe in the bathroom mirror earlier today," I answered. Despite this, we got on very well, which may have something to do with the Marvel goody bag I presented him with. I was invited down to his home studio the following week. His house was typical rockstar domain. Suits of armour stood between pinball machines.

Entering the studio, Brian handed me THE guitar and suggested I play. Unworthy doesn't come close. He flipped a few levers and dials and his brand new Spider-Man theme blasted out of the speakers. It was and is like nothing I have ever heard before or since. Amazing Spider-Man. As Brian's guitar let rip, images of Spidey skittering around the walls and ceiling of the studio came to mind.

And so we came to launch day for the radio series. It had already garnered more media interest and press attention than anything else created by Marvel UK. I was about to head out to the launch event when, passing through the Marvel foyer I was stopped by The Boss. "Why are we bothering with this radio nonsense?" he asked. Now this radio nonsense had taken a lot of work outside office hours from myself. Also, it was a brilliant idea. So I was a little put out by the moronic question and answered slowly so that even an amoeba would get my drift: "To…promote…our…product…so…people…buy…it." Our attractive young receptionist couldn't resist laughing out loud at this. My boss gave me the I'll kill you, you bastard look beloved of all Victorian mill owners.

The launch was a blast, again attracting a lot of media interest. The first episode of the drama was played to great effect. Back at the office, I found an envelope waiting on my desk. It was my first Letter of Warning. Now you don't want to get a Letter of Warning no matter where you work, but for some reason I could not take this one seriously. For one thing, it had Spider-Man and the Incredible Hulk rampaging across the top of the letterhead. I pinned it up on the main office wall so all my fellow Marvelites could see. The Boss spotted it, pulled it down and banged it back on my desk warning: "Take it seriously!" "I can't!" I replied. "I'm going for the three!" (3 Letters of Warning and you are out).

Later that week, my boss entered my office and closed the door behind him. He shook his head as he looked at me.
"You know your problem, Tim?"
"No, can't say I do. Pray tell."
"You don't know the meaning of the word hierarchy."

"You're right. I come from Liverpool where we pride ourselves on not knowing the meaning of that word. If I wanted to understand it I would be working for a non-creative company rather than Marvel Comics."

Hmm. The writing was obviously on the wall.

And then I got a call from Andrew Lloyd Webber's office. They wanted to see me about an idea I had mailed to them months before. So a few days later I found myself sitting opposite Andrew at his London office. My idea was simple. A musical featuring Marvel comic book characters. Andrew had already taken the unlikely character of the Phantom of the Opera and turned him into a world- wide musical success. He told me that the Marvel idea appealed to him as he saw the romance in normal people being turned into super-heroes, donning skintights, masks and capes and attempting to keep the secret from their girl or boy friend. Andrew asked which of our characters I thought would work best on stage. I told him that some would prove to be impossible to work with such as the Human Torch due to theatre Health & Safety fire restrictions and Submariner due to the impossibility of showing the undersea world on stage. He stopped me before I could go any further. "Neither of those would be a problem for us. We can do anything on stage." Well I liked the sound of that. Andrew suggested I compile a list of which heroes weren't bound to movie or TV deals and come back with my boss in a week's time to push the idea onwards. Sounded good to me. I headed back to the office and told my boss the exciting news. He merely nodded and put it down in his diary. I told him to get the information from New York as to just which characters we would be able to hand over to ALW.

Cut ahead one week. Back in Andrew's office. I introduce my boss. Pleasantries. Tea poured. Andrew: "So which of your characters can I use?" I turn to my boss. "Ahh, I haven't found out yet," he replies. SILENCE as Andrew digests this, his face getting redder as he does so. "Then why are we having this meeting? Call me when you have the details." And up and out of the office goes Andrew. As we leave the building my boss turns to me with a heavy sigh and says, "Do you have any idea how much work this will involve?"

Time to move on...But first, I had wanted to produce a humour magazine for some time at Marvel, but I didn't want it to end up looking and reading like the countless Viz rip-offs. There was a TV series called The Comic Strip that seemed an ideal match. The producer, writer and main actor of the series was a chap by the name of Peter Richardson. Peter liked the idea of collaborating with Marvel especially as he had a brand new series about to launch on the BBC. He asked me to accompany him on a trip to talk with the management at BBC TV Centre. He wanted to show them that Marvel Comics was interested in the series.

On the way across London Peter kept noticing huge billboards advertising a new series coming up from Robbie Coltraine. "Why aren't the BBC doing this with my series?" he asked. I could feel his rage grow as we checked in at BBC reception. By the time we were in the meeting and the BBC executives were smiling nicely and pouring tea in their best china, Peter was like a rumbling volcano beside me. And then he blew. It was a real explosion. Months and months of pent up frustration with his bosses spewed out. I could relate to this. He finished by crashing both hands down on the table top causing cups, saucers, milk, tea and biscuits to shoot skywards. And then he strode magnificently from the room, slamming the door behind him. I wanted to applaud but there was that slightly embarrassing moment where I looked around at the execs and they looked back at me. Obviously they couldn't speak while I was still there and so I nodded farewell and went in search of Peter.

He was in a better mood during the few script sessions we had together with his cast, which included the model and author Sara Stockbridge. The magazine was an interesting project but I didn't stay to see it through. Back at Marvel I had had a call from a publisher called Richard Desmond. He was thinking about starting up a comic book department within his company and wondered whether I wanted to head it up. As I was feeling about Marvel much the same way Peter Richardson was feeling about the BBC, and also because my salary would immediately be tripled, I accepted the job. Peter's series, 'Glam Metal Detectives', came out and was barely noticed thanks to the BBC's crafty scheduling and lack of promotion. Marvel put out a Glam Metal Detectives mag that looked and read just like all the other Viz rip-offs.

Ugh!

And so on to Richard Desmond's company out at Docklands. Richard, or Dirty Des as Private Eye have branded him, had recently launched 'OK' magazine and wanted to show he was a family publisher to get away from the image created by his top-shelf publications. We were to launch 3 titles. Power Rangers, Action Man, and Sindy. My first day in the job and I knew I'd made a mistake. Not so much in leaving Marvel as in signing on with RD. I've now sat here for half an hour attempting to think of things I can write about that company and that man that won't see me in court. I was there 3 months. I ended up being escorted from the building by a security man. I loathed every minute and my flesh crawls at the memories. And so I draw a veil over those 3 months of my life out at Docklands...

Melvyn Bragg

...And head off to Nashville. I'd kept in with my friends over at LWT's South Bank Show and pitched the idea of making a documentary on women in Country Music. At this moment in time a lot of excellent female singer/songwriters were coming out of Nashville. I thought it would be interesting to find out just how they coped in what was predominantly a redneck scene. So, film crew in hand, I jumped aboard one of the first direct flights to Nashville to meet and interview the names of the day. Mary Chapin Carpenter, Kathy Mattea, Pam Tillis, Suzy Bogguss, and the rest. The trip coincided with that year's televised Country Music Awards where I found myself in the celebrity-filled audience sitting behind Julia Roberts and her husband Lyle Lovett. As well as the big names, I thought we should try and showcase a new act on the programme.

With this in mind I went on the Gerry House Show at a local radio station. I mentioned that if any new female singer/songwriters were out there they could meet me at Tootsie's Bar Lounge at 1pm that day and to bring a cassette of their work. Sitting in the bar later on I was disappointed at 1:05pm to find nobody had bothered showing until a woman put her head round a doorway at the back of the room and asked: "Are you the English guy? There're about 100 girls waiting for you back here." And so there were. And every one of them had a cassette tape. And every one of them was good if not better than good. I ended up throwing the tapes in the air and featuring the one I caught. Careers are made on such moves!

Melvyn Bragg was a joy to work for. You would pitch the idea for a show and he would give you an instant yes or no. If yes, you'd work out a budget and timescale for filming and editing the show. In the case of the Nashville show the budget was £80,000. The whole thing was a fairly simple operation. I'd make contact with the various people I wanted in the programme, set up a time to film an interview with each of them, and attempt to build a cohesive story that would run for 50+minutes. Once the editing process was complete, Melvyn would come down and view the rough edit deep beneath LWT's tower block on the banks of the Thames. He would scribble notes as he watched, tearing the pages from his book to hand to me at the end. They were always simple but very effective changes to pull the edit together. That was it. My kind of boss.

Enid Blyton's Mystery & Suspense

Back in the UK, Enid Blyton was about to celebrate her 100th birthday. At least she would have been had she still been alive. Regardless of this small matter, the publisher Egmont Fleetway decided to launch a brand new Enid Blyton weekly. Enid's elder daughter, Gillian, suggested me for the job of editor. Although we had never got round to publishing the Enid Blyton comic at Marvel, Gillian and I had got on very well and shared much the same view about her Mum's amazing work.

So there I am and all is well on Day 1 at Egmont Fleetway. It only started going downhill from Day 2. The company wanted the magazine to tie in to a new TV series based on Blyton's Famous Five stories. Fair enough. Good idea even, except that they wanted the rest of the magazine to be made up of Enid's other kids-go-after-crooks tales. This was guaranteed to make the magazine a little samey from page to page. I would much rather have featured a variety of Blyton's tales from Fairy Tale type stories to nature, school, Robin Hood and dog exploits. Oh well, I attempted to make sure the illustrator's for each story would be completely different to each other, which would give some variety. Egmont had already come up with the name 'Enid Blyton's Mystery & Suspense'. With this in mind, I commissioned a dark and brooding cover for issue Number One showing the Famous Five in dire straits in a rowing boat on a stormy ocean as an old fashioned galleon is hurled up from the depths and lit by a flash of lightning. Mario Capaldi turned in a stupendous piece of art, which everybody in the office was blown away by. You actually got drenched if you stood too near the painting. Two days later, the picture was pulled as being too dark and gloomy to be the cover of a first issue. "We want something bright and fun," I was told. "But the title is Mystery & Suspense," I argued. "Surely that means dark and spooky?" Apparently not.

Now my wife Jane had told me to make sure I just nod during editorial meetings from now on, and take the cheque at the end of the month. That had been my intent on arriving at Egmont. But...sitting in an early editorial meeting I was told by the Head of Marketing that she had just been in conversation with the Marketing Dept at Sainsburys. They had told her that they had put a yellow stripe down the edge of their generic brand of All Bran and it had caused a huge increase in sales. "So I suggest you put a yellow stripe down the edge of the comic, Tim." I nodded. To be honest, it was all I could do as I was without speech. The HoM did a double-take at me. "What's up?" "What do you mean?" I asked. "That look on your face," she answered. Betrayed by my own face. It was at that moment I realized I was in a place Enid Blyton had created many years' previously. She called it The Land of Stupids.

I'd been promised that Egmont would be putting on a huge promotion for the launch. One month from D Day I raised the subject again. I was told that the plan had been changed. We were going to launch the magazine with zero promotion and wait six months until we knew who our readership was so that we could then aim our promotions directly at that group. "But we already know that a large percentage of our audience will be Enid Blyton readers," I protested. "Shouldn't we let them know?" Nope. We would wait six months. Sound stupid to you? Me too.

Speaking of the launch, I suggested organizing a Launch Party. For some unknown reason this was agreed to but I was told to only invite important people to the party. "Yeah, our contributors," I said. "No, not them," explained my Group Leader. "Just the printers and marketing department." That day I mailed out invitations to every illustrator and writer I had ever worked with.

One of these was Jemima Rooper. She was a fourteen year-old actress who was playing the part of George the tomboy in the ITV Famous Five series. I'd already interviewed her and asked her to adapt one of Blyton's stories for the mag. She turned in a superb adaptation that captured the visual elements of the story perfectly. Jemima was a very natural writer. She agreed to write regularly for the magazine. When I told my Group Leader back at Egmont he asked her age. "Fourteen? Great we can give her a child's rate." Bloody typical. There are so few good writers in comic books and here was one we should have been encouraging. Not that it really mattered as Jemima has gone on to a golden career, starring on TV, in the West End and on Broadway. Child's rate! Idiot!

And it gets worse. Another management bozo at Egmont suggested I make one of the Famous Five black. "No problem," I said. "But we shall have to make them all black as they are all from the same family." This wouldn't do, of course, so the Famous Five remained as Blyton had created them 40+ years earlier.

The launch was fun. Denis Gifford, comics historian and writer and illustrator, turned up and deemed the mag the best children's periodical he had seen in over a decade. He was right in my modest opinion. The magazine featured the talents of Phil Gascoine, Mario Capaldi, Maureen & Gordon Gray, John Lupton, and Steve Parkhouse. TV's Famous Five turned up that night too, and I seem to remember that either Dick or Julian became a little inebriated by the end of the party. Obviously overdoing the lashings of Ginger Beer.

The magazine came out and the cunning plan of Egmont worked. Nobody was aware it was there. Bewilderingly, a member of staff confided in me that it was really important for two high ups at Egmont that the mag should fail as they had launched a magazine the previous year that had flopped and it would look bad for them if this one soared. As I've found way too many times in management, you couldn't make it up. By issue 7, I was called into the Marketing Director's office to be told I was going to be let go.

"Are you canning the mag?" I asked.

"No, it shall keep on running."

"Will you be changing it?"

"No. Everybody loves what you have done with it."

"Then why are you firing me?"

"Because we have to be seen to be doing something in light of the poor sales."

I kid you not. Those were the exact words because I wrote them down immediately after, knowing I wouldn't believe it a day later. Foolishly they gave me the option of going that moment or one week later so that I could hand the mag over to the new editor. I chose to stay on as I had a plan. The following day I contacted every contributor I had ever used and told them to supply me with as much Enid Blyton material as they could over the next few days. Soon as it came in I signed each invoice and sent it up to Accounts. By the time I left the company had enough Blyton material to keep them going over the next two years, which was a shame as the mag only lasted another three issues. Oh dear. What a shame. By this time I was wondering what I was doing in the comic book business. It wasn't much fun anymore. I remember my Group Editor at Egmont looking over a strip page of art roughs from that master Mario Capaldi and circling 42 different points on the page for correction. She claimed his body work was all off. It wasn't, but this was another example of somebody needing to be seen to be doing something.

Blue Moon

I was back in the US working for The Saturday Evening Post Magazine again as editor on their US Kids magazine when I got a fax from Gillian Baverstock. She was Enid Blyton's elder daughter and we had kept in touch since working on the Marvel Blyton dummy. Gillian suggested we team-up and form our own publishing company to put out comic books that would encourage a love of reading in children. Seemed like a great idea to me, so we loaded up the truck and moved to Shrewsbury in Shropshire. The house we chose was massive to serve as both living area and editorial offices. The staircase in the house was from the 1500's so would have matched the Marvel UK chimneypots.

We called the new company Quill Publications, Quill being an amalgam of the name Quinn and Gill. It was decided that our first magazine would be a series of sequels to fairy tales, myths and legends featuring such characters as Jack of the Beanstalk, Puss in Boots, Aladdin, Tom Thumb, Cinderella, Rumpelstiltskin, Medusa, Snow White, Sleeping Beauty, Red Riding Hood, and the Pied Piper. All these characters lived in the same town so they would often bump into each other during their adventures. The whole comic was pulled together by two modern day kids and their dog who could witness these adventures through their Amazing Computer. It turned out that the boy was actually the once and future king Arthur. I brought in a variety of illustrators from Marvel Comics and other places I'd worked both in the UK and the US. Gillian, Jane and I wrote the stories. We also included beautifully illustrated poetry and history pages. The idea was to plant seeds of interest in a variety of subjects in our readers.

The whole thing came together over a six-month period and looked great. This was definitely a project that could develop in any number of interesting ways. We brought in a distribution company who promised they would get us into every possible outlet across the UK. BBC Radio 4 created a programme to follow us from initial idea to launch and beyond. The media caught on and were keen to promote the idea of a guy from Marvel teaming up with the daughter of Enid Blyton. Gillian's writing was great, certainly in line with her Mum's. We came up with the name 'Blue Moon' for the comic. This was the name of the land where the characters lived.

The week leading up to the launch had stories in most of the national newspapers. On launch day the BBC Radio 4 programme suggested they record Gillian and I as we headed into the Sloane Square WH Smiths to pick up our copy of the published comic. Great idea. Except. It. Wasn't. There. Microphone in our faces as we were asked how this made us feel. Phone call to our distributor who asks: "Are you sure it's not there? It should be." We were sure. It wasn't there. Nor was it there the next day or the day after that. It finally arrived four days late thanks to the skill of our distribution company. This made all our promotions pointless. Customers might go back on the second day. Maybe even the third, but no way would they still be looking on day 4. And it was the same problem up and down the country. Similar story with the following issue. Two days late. And issue 3. The distributor assured us each time that this problem would be sorted but it never was. However, the readers who were picking up the comic loved it. We started getting letters from teachers who were using it during Literacy Hour. Parents, grandparents and, most important of all, children themselves loved the stories. The letters were very heartening. But the sales simply didn't pick up enough after the fiasco of the launch issue.

We got an email from Stan Lee who had seen the first three issues. He liked them and told us about the new website he had just launched and that there might be room for a possible linkup to Blue Moon. Well that was exciting. Not quite as exciting as when Stan's website went bust a very short time later, but still exciting. The comic looked better with each edition, and so we plodded on from issue to issue, lifted up by letters from readers and brought down by sales figures. It simply wasn't catching on fast enough. 36 brand new pages every issue cost a lot to produce. Slowly but surely we were sinking. After issue 12 we sunk. It was a tough week. On the Monday Jane's mother died. On the Tuesday our company went belly-up and we lost everything including our house. I spoke with my Dad on the phone that night and he gave me the Dad advice: "Never mind, son. You've got your health." Unfortunately, the following day Jane was diagnosed with a brain tumour. This was really turning out to be a very bad week indeed.

Life is what happens while you are busy making other plans

What can I tell you after that? Everything changed. Everything. As John Lennon once said, life is what happens while you are busy making other plans. To prove his point he then went and got himself shot. Nothing quite so drastic here. For the next two years we lived in a garden shed. Honest. Admittedly the garden shed was in a millionaire belt outside London and our neighbours were rock and pop stars from the Sixties, but it was still a bloody garden shed. Jane went through various hellish depleting operations, the after effects, which still shudder through to this day. I suspect we both went a bit nuts because in the midst of all this we formed our own management company and started working with musicians and bands putting on tours, concerts and charity shows. An interesting bunch of characters they were too with Bill Wyman, Donovan, Albert Lee, John Paul Jones, Kiki Dee, Julie Felix, Steve Harley & Cockney Rebel to name but a few crossing our musical path. Happily we were no longer living in a garden shed but rather back where I once belonged in Merseyside. All roads lead to Home.

And Merseyside now had its own television station, Bay TV Liverpool. Sitting over a cuppa or two with good friend and musician of musicians Craig LW, we got talking about our love of the Mersey Beat period from the early Sixties. On the spot we determined to set off and interview many of the surviving 'groups' from that time. On a whim we strolled over to Bay TV and sold them the idea on the spot. So for the last few months we have had the delightful job of interviewing our heroes in front of the telly cameras capturing amazing tales from that most heady of decades. Total joy to be compiling these stories and editing them into a series of documentaries. We are also filming complete concerts featuring these artists down in Liverpool's legendary Cavern Club. They can still blast it out, fifty years on! At heart, I'd always wanted to be a Beatle but missed the boat when they were hiring, so this is as close as I'm likely to get.

And speaking of history, one of the highlights of 2015 was being contacted by Miwk Publishing who wanted to gather together the Doctor Who strips produced by Dicky Howett and myself back in the dawn of time. I don't think that either of us had been aware of how many of these strips we had done. And some of them were actually funny! The first print run has just sold out. Shocked and stunned doesn't come close. It's only taken me 45 years to find a publisher who knows what they are doing. You've got to laugh.

I do keep a hand in magazines these days. About ten years ago I realized that there were no longer any magazines on the newsstands that I bought each month. This came as a shock because along with comic books I had always loved various magazines for their style and personality. Suddenly there was no periodical I couldn't wait to come out each month. The newsstands looked dull and stupid with covers blazing the delights of X-Factor or other trash programmes. Gillian Baverstock suggested I rectify this by heading into schools and finding the next generation of journalists. She had noticed that very few schools had school magazines these days. That seemed nuts as these gave opportunities for non-academic students to shine in their own way.

So during the last decade I have been going into schools across the UK and working with editorial teams of students to produce brand new general interest magazines. The intent is that they will look and read as good as anything on the newsstands (that's not difficult). My aim is to be able to take a copy of these magazines and hand it to someone in New York or Sydney and for them to immediately want to know when the next edition is coming out. I'm very proud of the work of my students. The magazines shine out in comparison to the tripe put out by professional publishers, and it is the work of kids. They put their heart, soul and humour into these magazines and there is the difference. Many famous names have helped support this venture by allowing me to take groups of students to interview them. All of these names have been blown away by the resulting magazine. Sir Tim Rice, Jeffrey Archer, Jeremy Paxman, Melvyn Bragg, Willy Russell, Helen Skelton, David Morrissey, Bill Wyman, Deborah Meaden, Julian Clary, Eddie Izzard, and the list goes on… Are there comic strips in these magazines? But of course! The story continues…

END

The Bit After the End

Yeah, that meant to be the end but then the memories wouldn't stop coming. Moments in time would suddenly flash into sharp relief. I'd scribble them down as fast as they came. There seemed to be no continuity to them. At one moment I'd be in 1975 and the next it would be 2018 before leaping back to 1958 and 1999. My life had become a series of dreams and I'd like to present a few of those moments in the closing chapter......

You've Go to Laugh

Back in 2001, Jane developed a brain tumour. This is quite as ghastly as it sounds. Our life was turned upside down with the click of an x-ray. We were sent to what was called a 'centre of excellence' in Stoke-on-Trent (oxymoron, surely?) to meet the surgeon at a hospital that was once a Victorian lunatic asylum. He did the usual grim thing of detailing everything that could go wrong while admitting "We don't really know anything about the brain." Not exactly instilling confidence. The eight hour operation seemed to go on for 80 years as I paced the hospital corridors. The surgeon's first words to me afterwards were "Unfortunately we tore the lining to the brain." By this stage I was on the ground but he assured me all was well with the patch up job they had quickly stitched up. During that week, I noticed that every other patient who went in for a similar operation came out as a basket case. Jane after many very painful days due to unnecessary insertion of needles into her spine, came round and by the fifth day I was able to read the newspaper to her. Unfortunately the lead story was a report that George Harrison had just been diagnosed with a brain tumour.

Six months went by and we went back to the hospital for a routine scan to make sure the tumour hadn't regrown. They hadn't been able to take the whole damn thing out because it had grown round the main artery to the brain. Great news. All was well. No regrowth. Hooray! 2 weeks later Jane told me that she felt that the tumour was re-growing because she was feeling similar symptoms with her vision that had tipped us off first time round. I attempted to jolly her along not wanting to believe the worst. Then we got a call from the hospital. They had given us the wrong readings and they now found that the tumour was indeed re-growing. This was another moment that changed everything in our life. I can still feel the vibration.

Disgusted with the whole scene at this 'centre of excellence', I Googled brain surgeons and found that a man called Michael Powell was rated as the 2nd greatest brain surgeon in the world. And he operated out of London. I somehow managed to get him on the phone and we were invited to meet at his office. We loved him as soon as we met. On the wall behind his desk was a framed version of this photo. He explained that he had operated on Michael Palin's wife a short while before. Over the moon at the results, the Monty Python star asked the surgeon if there was anything he could do to thank him. "Yes," replied Mr Powell. This photo was the result. That's Michael Powell, Jane's brain surgeon on the right, with Palin on the left.

As Jane has always said through thick and thin: "You've got to laugh." Without a doubt Mr Powell saved her life for which we are eternally grateful.

Gyles Brandreth

Now here's a guy who should be running the planet. He is always working on a thousand new projects from creating a Teddy Bear Museum to teaming up with me to create Sherlock Holmes graphic novels for Collins Books. Sheer joy working with him over a couple of years. We laughed a lot!

And his political diaries are well worth a read to see just why there is no hope for anything to work under the current ghastly system and equally ghastly parties.

One day we were guest speakers at the 600th anniversary of a school. We encouraged each other to drop 'inappropriate' lines into our speeches. He kicked off by claiming that he had been harassed by explicit texts from the Headmaster's wife during the last week. This went over like a lead balloon to our joy.

Naughty But Nice

Back in my teens working at the City Varieties in Leeds, I soon knew all the lyrics to the risqué songs once sung by that Queen of the Music Halls Marie Lloyd. My favourite was a delightful little ditty titled 'She Sits Amongst the Cabbages and Peas'. The Puritans of Great Britain rose up as one when she first sang the number and caused such a ruckus that she agreed to change the lyric. Next night she went on stage she sang the new version: 'She Sits Amongst the Cabbages and Leeks'.

Fabs

I don't know how this is, and I'm sure I'm not the only one to feel this way, but every so often I hear a Beatle track and it's as if I'm hearing it for the very first time, despite the fact that it is more likely to be the ten thousandth listening. The last 3 minutes it was Penny Lane that had this uplifting and energising impact. I remember hearing it for the first time back in January 1967 but today it was back fresh as a daisy. How on Earth? I'm tempted to ask what were they on, but we all know what they were on; with most people that just makes them write airy-fairy high-as-a-kite gibberish. This is storytelling at its best. I remember Penny Lane, the place, pre-Beatles. We had an old Aunt who lived just off it and we used to regularly visit the Abbey cinema. I certainly don't remember being inspired by the area's poetic possibilities. I guess that's where genius comes in. Or witchcraft. Either way works for me. For the billionth time: Thanks, Beatles.

Overture and Beginners, Please

It was 1970, and I didn't like the way things were shaping up in the brand new decade. I'd loved the Sixties. What was there not to love? Four Feather Falls, Doctor Who, Bootsie & Snudge, Arthur Haynes, Scene at 6:30, Billy Cotton, Juke Box Jury, TV21, new-fangled felt tip pens, sweet cigarettes. Ahh, sweet cigarettes! Just like the Home Service they have been renamed for the modern world. Candy sticks. We don't want to encourage children to smoke these days, do we? How sweet to have grown up in a world where you could become a twenty-a-day sweet ciggy sucker by the age of six. And that was only the beginning, for every Christmas you could be sure to find a Smoker's Set tucked in your stocking. This comprised chocolate cigarettes, matches, cigars, pipe and ashtray. And that drug of the schoolboy masses, Sweet Tobacco. Can you taste it? If you were there 60+ years ago then I know you can as it's a taste that lingers regardless of Gibbs SR. They sure wanted you to smoke back then.

But that was then and this was 1970 and the Beatles had just split. Life's all downhill after the Beatles split and with the horrors of so-called Glam Rock waiting in the wings I needed to escape. And so I did to the 1880's. It was a very easy route, just like stepping through the wardrobe to Narnia. Off the main street of Leeds and down a particularly dirty, dustbin lined alleyway to the Stage Door of the City Varieties Music Hall in search of a job. As the door closed behind me, a wolf came crashing down the staircase in front of me.

"Bugger! Bugger! BUGGER!" he raged, picking himself up. "I can't see a bloody thing out of this stupid head! Is my tail on?" I checked. It wasn't. "Be a love and run upstairs and see if I've left it on the dressing room table. I'm in the Empire, second door along."

Simple enough directions but I somehow got lost in the Green Room where a hunchbacked old scrote was applying boot-blacking to his hair, surrounded by Gorgeous Gaiety Girls and a Little Red Riding Hood who was bursting out all over. "Who the hell are you?" asked the scrote who was in fact Wally, the Stage Manager. I found this to be his normal enquiry of any new face.

"I'm looking for the wolf's tail...in the Empire..." I explained.

"Never mind that idiot's tail, we need you in the Limes. The show's about to start," said Wally.

"What's the Limes?"

"For God's sake! Do I have to do everything myself?" With polish blackened hands he pushed me up three staircases and across a musty storeroom to the Limes.

"Are you wearing rubber soles?" asked Wally, flipping a huge master switch to set an ancient spotlight in motion. "It's just that it's been playing up a bit."

There was no Health & Safety back in 1970. A Frankenstein-like burst of energy exploded into blinding life by the touching of two carbon rods and my mighty machine lit up the stage down below. The curtain rose and out stepped the Wolf to sing the very risqué opener:

"How could Red Riding Hood Have been so very good And still keep the Wolf from the door..?"

I was home.

The Funniest Man in the Universe. Ken Dodd.
"Ger yer haircut, Quinn! You'll never get anywhere in this
business with hair like that!"

Managing Julie Felix. "Can we get a working toilet in this
dressing room?" The glamour of showbiz.

116

Direct from the set of TV's Supergirl and Grey's Anatomy to a
charity concert at Liverpool's Cavern Club. The splendid
Chyler Leigh.

Mike McGear McCartney and I share a brolly as we set out for
the first date in his theatre tour of the UK. By the end of the
tour we were both in agreement as to whose fault it was that it
flopped.

Exhibit 'A', m'lud.

ANGER OVER COMIC 'SMUT'

POLICE in Hanley belive that a children's comic could be breaking "obscenity" laws.

They are sending a report and a copy of the comic—"Channel 33½"—to the Metropolitan Police for possible action against the publishers, Marvel Comics.

The move comes after a furious Kidsgrove father complained that the comic he bought for his 11-year-old son contained "bad language" and pictured glue sniffing and copulation.

Mr. Derek James, of Ianroad, Newchapel, alleged: "The comic is full of glue sniffing, prostitution, mass murder—and includes a couple copulating.

"I am not naive .... but I think the comic is diabolical. It is wrong to feed very young kids this sort of material."

Mr. James, aged 45, who bought "Channel 33½" at a Hartshill newsagent's, was particularly upset by its cover billing as a "Children's Comic."

"I only discovered what it was like inside when my son asked me whether a certain word was rude. Other parents may still be ignorant as to what is inside the covers."

Said a senior detective in Hanley today: "We will be forwarding a report and a copy of the comic to the Metropolitan Police for their consideration under the Children and Young Persons (Harmful Publications) Act."

He said that this procedure was necessary because the publishers were based in London. He added that any prosecution under the Act would require the consent of the Attorney-General.

A spokesman for Marvel Comics said: "It is not our policy to publish anything which would corrupt children."

Seduction of the Innocent

What Happened in 1769? Find Out With Tim Tyme!

121

THE AMAZING SPIDER-MAN

Starring

WILLIAM DUFRIS as................Peter Parker/Spider-Man
LORELEI KING as................Sue Storm/Betty Brant
WILLIAM ROBERTS as................J Jonah Jameson/Uncle Ben
PETER MARINKER as................Reed Richards
BUFFY DAVIS as................Aunt May
JONATHAN KYDD as................The Green Goblin
GARY MARTIN as........The Thing/Ben Grimm/The Dread Dormammu
GARRICK HAGON as................Prince Namor, The Sub-Mariner
ERIC MEYERS as................Johnny Storm/The Human Torch
DAVID BANNERMAN as................Flash Thompson
MICHAEL ROBERTS as................Doctor Doom/Sandman
SIMON TREVES as................Doctor Octopus
and
ANITA DOBSON as................Liz Allan

Edited by Tim Quinn. Published by Marvel Comics. Original music composed and performed by Mark Russell. Audio adaptation written and directed by Dirk Maggs.

Spider-Man theme composed and performed by Brian May. Published by Queen Music Limited. Produced by Brian May and Justin Shirley-Smith.

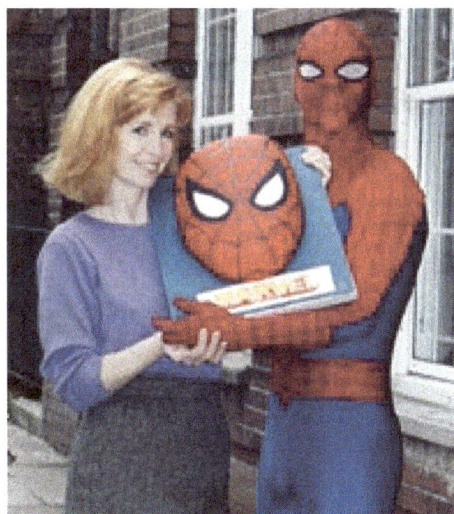

Jane Asher and Spider-Cake 1

123

Arundel House, 13/15 Arundel Street, London WC2R 3DX
Telephone 071-497 2121. Fax 071-497 2234.

MEMORANDUM

FROM: PAUL NEARY
TO: TIM QUINN

CC: MIKE HOBSON
         CAROLINE AUBREY

DATE: 13 JANUARY 1995

Please take this as your first warning. Three such warnings will
result in dismissal. I'm sure I don't need to tell you that
continuation of your behaviour at noon today in the front hall can
have only one outcome.

Reg. Office 100 Chalk Farm Road, London NW1. Reg. No. 1034747 VAT No. GB 232 5088 74

This delight has hung proudly on my office wall ever since.
Can't please all the people all the time.

QUEEN

Tim Quinn
Marvel Comics Ltd
Arundel House
13-15 Arundel Street
London WC2R 3DX

11 February 1993

Dear Tim,

Thanks for the great books, which I am perusing avidly. It is a very inspiring thought, and I have a feeling that it may be a great collaboration. Anyone with a letter head like yours must be worth talking to !

Cheers,

Brian May

let's talk....!

[signature: Brian May]

Gillian Baverstock, elder daughter of Enid Blyton, and Bruce the dog at the doorway to our publishing house for 'Blue Moon'.

The Great Marvel Comics Float with waterlogged super-heroes in the pouring rain.

The day Alice Cooper popped in to visit the Marvel Comics offices.

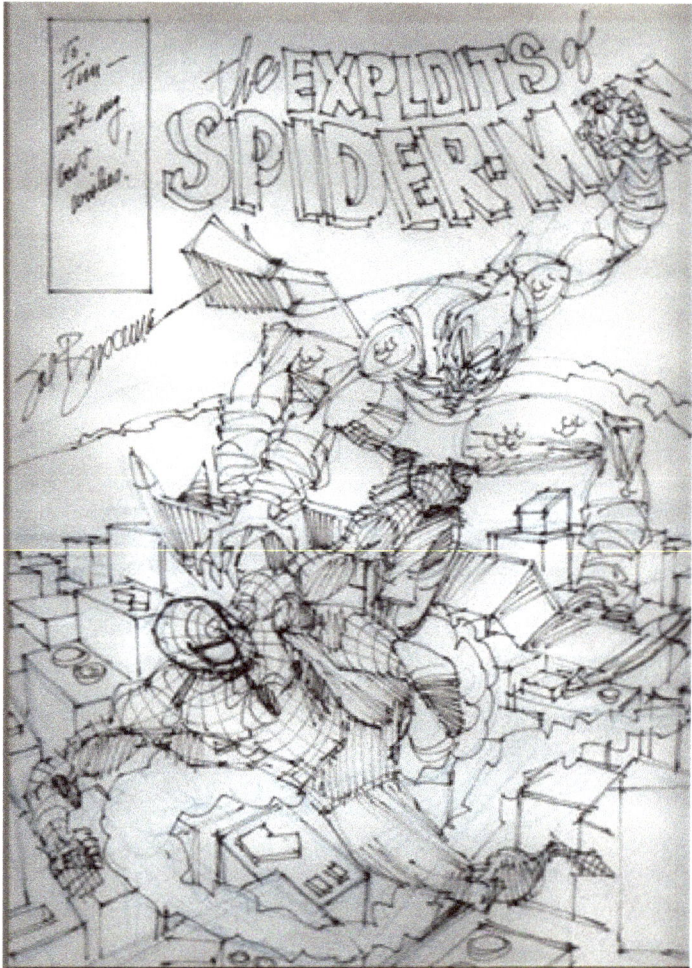
Cover rough sketch from Sal Buscema

Steve Parkhouse frenzy

1997 – Enid Blyton's TV Famous Five with Timmy the dog and Timmy the Editor.

The Sherlock Homes Irregulars
With the one and only Gyles Brandreth

With Queen Victoria herself, Jenna Coleman, after we realise
that the organiser of the Comic Con has slipped off with the
takings before paying us.

Captain Audible Dirk Maggs

Brian May and Spidey atop BBC Broadcasting House to promote our Marvel/BBC radio drama

Today – Curating with former Beatle Pete Best and his brother
Roag Aspinall Best at the Liverpool Beatles Museum

Today – Bringing comics to kids with Liverpool Heartbeat

Hooray!

56 years ago I was cheering Victorian adventurer Adam
Adamant and his dolly bird assistant, Miss Georgina. It was an
amazing concept that a man from 65 years ago was plodding
around in the Swinging London of 1966.

A few more years and I will know exactly how he felt. Last
night I was sitting on a train returning from town with a
Liverpool Dolly Bird opposite me. She was engrossed in the
medical operation of glueing on huge Ming the Merciless style
finger nails. "Aw fuck! Me glue's run out and I still have two
nails to do. You got any nail glue, Mister?" Glueless, I offered
chewy, which got a laugh. But I could feel my Victorian
sensibilities tingling.

Every Picture Tells a Story

And this is a doozy. Mighty Quinn Management has been involved in many an odd project down the years to promote various charities. For MAG, the landmine clearance charity, we had organised a huge Ebay auction where celebrities sent in their shoes for bidding. The idea being to represent that every 10 minutes someone on this planet has their feet blown off by a bloody landmine. We got a lot of shoes from Ringo to Ken Russell and Pete Townshend and Alice Cooper. On launch day it was arranged that Heather Mills McCartney would be our spokesperson to the world's press at this spot on Carnaby Street.

All went well ... until Heather turned up. We got there early and set up the shoes in dramatic style. The media arrived by the score. A very happy crowd. And then Heather turned up. In a scene straight out of Ab Fab, she strode onto the set and slung a coat from her shoulders to drop across the head of her PA. The flustered PA then came over and explained to us that Heather would not be speaking and nor would she be taking questions. Instead, she stood there in front of the shoes with a face of thunder. Look! There it is caught for all time. The press, expecting words of wisdom and a Q&A turned icy cold on the spot. I don't think she was ever treated with any respect by them after this incident. The photographers took a few shots but not a single editor chose to use the picture or story the next day. So thanks a lot, Heather.

A learning curve for Mighty Quinn Management. Choose your spokesperson very carefully. A refrigerator would have had more charm.

Good God

A wonderful morning was followed by a very reasonable early afternoon with emails and phone calls being returned in the positive. The sun was up and the sky was blue. And then it all changed. A shadow fell on my front path and rang on my door. It was two young men with briefcases, one Bible and a stack of Watchtowers. They were dressed identically in the kind of suits that give suits a bad name. They shared the same haircut. And they were very clean. Exceptionally so. My dog could have ate his dinner off them.

Despite the fact that they were born in the 1660's they were very young. There was something of the foetus about them. Their teeth were 100% American.

"Good afternoon, sir, What does the word morality mean to you?" asked Tweedledum.

To help me grasp the significance of the greeting, Tweedledee held up a copy of The Watchtower that had a cover shot of men, women and children burning and the word MORALITY superimposed over them. It was obviously a trick question, right? I'm no fool. So I quickly turned it back on them: "No, no, what does the word morality mean to you?" I will summarise their answer just in case you have a life. To the boys it meant salvation but also damnation for all those without morals. Ahh, this was my in. "Who are the people without morals?" I asked. "The evil people of the world," replied No. 1, actually beaming as he said it. "And who are they? Can you be specific?" Happily they could. "The people who don't follow the way of the Lord." "And what way is that?" "The way mapped out in The Bible." "But...but..." I protested, "I know lots of people who don't follow the path of The Bible. Some of them I even consider as friends. Does this mean they are doomed?" "Not if they open their hearts to the Lord. Let me read you a paragraph that covers this very point."

But before he could open the good book, I leapt in. "How old are you boys?" I lingered on the word boys." We are both twenty-four, sir," replied the well-mannered shit. "And do you consider that you have had many real life experiences in those twenty-four years? How long have you been away from the US?" They had been away for two months and they considered that their life experiences had come from Bible study. By now I felt I was channelling my Dad, a true Liverpudlian who believed that pretty much everybody deserved every opportunity in Life and Death whether they came with a bucketful of morals or were totally bankrupt. It is no coincidence that at age sixteen I chose to head off and live with the rogues and vagabonds of the circus and theatre world. The TV and publishing worlds were certainly a moral step down from that, and don't get me started on the musical world. Sheer bloody joyous real people living real lives, warts and all.

"I have a parable for you," I told my new friends of the doorstep. "I call it The Parable of Cliff Richard. Once, long ago, I was buying Cliff records. For this was 1961 and 1962 and I was a A Voice in the Wilderness before the plague of Beatles descended on the land. And then those same Beatles Pleased, Pleased Me although I was still ready to go on a Summer Holiday with Cliff and his pals. But then Cliff found Jesus and appeared on television on a Sunday evening religious show talking about morality and the lack of it in the showbiz world. And lo it came to pass that I never bought another Cliff Richard record. For I was smit with people who had life, soul, energy and mischief in their veins and Cliff no longer had these qualities." I was proud and happy with this parable though it fell on deaf ears probably because these two religious zealots had never heard of Cliff Richard whose only American hit, 'Devil Woman', hit the charts many years before their immaculate conception.

"Will you at least take a copy of The Watchtower to ponder?" they asked. "No, I hate the artwork and especially the crummy colouring," I answered. They looked truly offended at this, shrugged and buggered off. I've just seen them hours later coming back down the other side of the road. A kid riding past on a bike lobbed a Coke can to bounce off one of their heads. Bloody kids these days have no morals. Luckily they will all soon be in Hell.

Yggdrasil

Here it is. The World Tree. The Faraway Tree. It stands in the garden where I spent my childhood. Big brother Michael could shin up to the very top in a 1950's jiffy. I took a little longer...like hours. From the top you could see the ships a'sailing along the River Mersey and any passing Flying Saucers of which there were countless during that decade. And don't get me started on cigar shaped objects. We also had a tyre attached by rope to a branch of the tree on which we would swing till we touched the clouds.

I revisited our tree recently. The tyre and rope have long gone just like the two boys. And it is no longer climbable as the lowest branches are now 20 feet above my head. But we were there when we were all kids and knew how to reach for the sky.

Aimi MacDonald

Aimi Macdonald, or to give her her full title, 'The Lovely Aimi Macdonald' was the first Sixties Sex Symbol I encountered while working at Leeds City Varieties Music Hall in my impressionable teen years. She was impossibly cute with all the style and pizazz of a Twenties flapper. For a former Catholic schoolboy she had the unnerving habit of looking directly into your eyes when speaking to you. And speak to me she did. 'I have a quick change during my act. Can you be at the side of the stage to help me?' Despite never having spoken to a woman other than a nun or my Mother, I was nothing if not helpful and nodded in the affirmative.

To say I was all fingers and thumbs would be an understatement. The zip fastener on her sequinned bustier somehow got stuck by a curl of my luxurious locks. I was mortified as the orchestra replayed her entrance several times while the struggle went on backstage. Had I had an axe handy, I would have lopped off my head to get her back on stage.

Luckily, Aimi saw the funny side and started laughing uncontrollably. The MC went on and explained the predicament. I think I lost about 14 pounds in sweat in those appalling few minutes. Scissors ended up being used and Aimi got a roar of approval from the audience when she finally made her re-entrance. Bless her, she sought me out later and made me see the funny side with the words, 'It can't be easy working with a sex symbol like me.'

School

I've produced workshops in hundreds and hundreds of schools over the last 25 years. They have all worked remarkably well for the kids, teachers and myself.

All except this one from a few years ago...............

Unsettling start to the day. I was booked into a school to give a writing and drawing workshop to secluded students. I got a cab to the school from the railway station. The cab driver visibly flinched when I told him where I was going. "Rather you than me, mate."

I brushed the warning off having worked in hundreds of schools over the years and feeling I'd met every type of pupil. WRONG! I was heartened to hear that my first class comprised just 8 students from Year 9, and they were girls. What could possibly go wrong?

It went wrong from the moment they entered the room. A banshee screech so loud my brain is still ringing roared: "WTF's THAT? IT LOOKS LIKE A WOMAN!"

The 'it' in question was me. When my hearing returned I made light of the comment saying that it had been many years since I was last regularly mistaken for a woman during my extremely glamourous teen years. This and my seemingly calm demeanour did not go down well. "WTF's WRONG WITH IT? WHAT'S IT DOING HERE IN OUR CLASS? MISS, GET IT OUT!"

By now we were in the third minute of my 40 minute class and I was already counting the seconds. Rapier wit ensued between the pair of us. I also attempted to get the other 7 girls over onto my side but they were having none of it. Melodramatic yawning spread loudly across the class. I attempted a new tack: "Let's go round each of you and tell me what you love doing when you are outside the school. Maybe we can incorporate the things you love into a story. Laurie, would you like to start us off?"

"I like nuthin'!"

The other girls all had the exact same like. Two of them couldn't even be bothered voicing their loathing of all things and just shrugged with a puff of breath.

During that 40 minutes I tried every trick I have ever used to engage with kids of all ages. Result? Nuthin'. By the end of the lesson we were at a standoff with their frustration at life entwined with my frustration at not being able to communicate on any level with them.

After the lesson, the teacher congratulated me, "That's the first time I've seen them remain in the room through a whole lesson." I guess that's one box ticked but brings me little joy.

After break I had twelve Year 9 boys. Got 'em from the first second. They turned in fabulous work and came to shake my hand at the end of the lesson. I have no idea why this one worked and the first lesson didn't. I heard a few tales about the background of these children. The tales make your blood run cold. 14 years of age and in despair. Well done, education system.

All Along the Watchtower

I'm being hammered by the Jehovah's this year. Maybe I should just give in and sign up for an eternity of bliss. Today's doorstep challenge was the question: "Did Jesus exist?" I was asked this by Bob & Jocelyn who came brandishing an issue of The Watchtower's sister publication 'Awake!'

I decided the annoying intellectual response was best for my first broadside: "Do any of us really exist and more importantly, does it really matter either way?" I could tell from their WTF expressions that this line of enquiry was new to them and so I continued by reciting Ozymandius by Shelley, happy to find it still slips word perfect from my tongue 55 years since it caught my eye in a copy of 'Look & Learn':

I met a traveller from an antique land,
Who said—"Two vast and trunkless legs of stone
Stand in the desert. . . . Near them, on the sand,
Half sunk a shattered visage lies, whose frown,
And wrinkled lip, and sneer of cold command,
Tell that its sculptor well those passions read
Which yet survive, stamped on these lifeless things,
The hand that mocked them, and the heart that fed;
And on the pedestal, these words appear:
My name is Ozymandias, King of Kings;
Look on my Works, ye Mighty, and despair!
Nothing beside remains. Round the decay
Of that colossal Wreck, boundless and bare
The lone and level sands stretch far away.

I honestly have no idea what point I was trying to make with this recital other than making travellers to my door wish they'd never knocked. I brought Ebenezer Scrooge into the one-sided conversation by pointing out that he never actually existed but his tale has been a fine moral lesson for us all for nearly 200 years. Rounding off my sermon, I suggested that dogs were the true master race (dodgy Germanic choice of words there) as they were eternally happy with their lot, and that my own Scottie had never brought up the subject of religion with me over the water bowl.

"Ahh," said Jocelyn. "That's because dogs have no intellect."

Game, match and set to me, I think, as I told her to go in search of that mighty intellect in any history book from down through the ages.

I actually liked Bob and Jocelyn despite the silly sods not getting the glory of dogs. I could see them sitting with Richard Briers's Martin character down the pub over a shandy or two in Ever Decreasing Circles. We'd have probably have been the best of friends when we were two. I pointed out a neighbour to them. He was busy painting his gatepost. "Now there's a man in need of a path," I said. They both brightened. "No," I laughed. "He's actually as content as me." This news seemed to disappoint the pair but they shrugged it off with, "Well, we're not on that side of the road today anyway."

Beatle

While managing the singer Julie Felix, Jane and I organised a few charity concerts in aid of MAG, the landmine clearance organisation Princess Diana had been promoting just before her death. Look who turned up backstage at one of the events at the Royal Albert Hall!

Julie and Paul had been buddies since Julie's early appearances on David Frost's TV shows in the mid Sixties. At this point, Paul was married to Heather Mills, who, spotting we were having a laugh with her hubby, came over with a windchill factor of -36° and put a stop to such frivolity. Paul didn't exactly help himself by telling Heather: 'This is my old friend Julie from our glory days.' Without even a glimpse in Julie's direction, ol' hatchet face suggested they leave. I suspect Paul was taken home, severely thrashed and grounded for the next few months.

I've Just Seen a Face

So there we were, Mighty Quinn Management had been up and running for just over a year and already we were at the Royal Albert Hall in London. We were managing Julie Felix, Californian protest singer from the Sixties, and the show had been to protest about bleeding landmines being sold to all and sundry by our revolting governments. Now it was time for the after show party in the opulent back rooms of the Albert. (Fairly tatty back room actually). We're chatting away with Julie and Nanci Griffith when we hear a very, very familiar voice: "Julie!" We turn and it's him. Paul McCartney. Y'know, that fellah from The Beatles and Wings.

Julie and Paul embrace. It's been many a year since last they met. They try and figure out just when that was. 'Hey Jude' time? Maybe. And then Julie turns and introduces me: "Paul, this is Tim, my manager." Paul smiles and shakes my paw. I look into his eyes and all I can see is that face on all those LP covers I bought on day of release from NEMS record shop. Please, Please Me, With the Beatles, A Hard Day's Night, Beatles For Sale, Help, Rubber Soul, Revolver.... It's the same face I tell you! It's the same head round the face. I don't know exactly what I said to Paul on that occasion, certainly nothing comprehensible. The only thing that has come close in my life was when a thunderclap and lightning bolt exploded directly above my head during a major storm in 1979. It gave the feeling of there's more to this universe than meets the eye. A true force of nature. Anyhow, here are some photos from that night. That's Julie's noggin with the long black hair.

Behind the Red Door

Mighty Quinn Management was formed behind a huge Regency red door one day when I made the mistake of telling Sixties Folk/Rock singer Julie Felix that her agent was a cock. This was hardly news to her but in her frustration she bawled, "Then do a better job than him...please!"

I asked various friends in the business if they knew of a good agent or manager and they all reported back with the same line, "There's no such thing." So Jane and I gave it a go. Very successfully too in those early years. It was hardly brain surgery as we knew for a fact. It was enormous fun heading out on the road with Julie on our first 40+ date tour in fabulous theatres and art centres across the UK. And then we had the brainwave to put together a double album of Dylan classics and pull in some of Julie's old Sixties pals on support. I remember sitting round Julie's dinner table late at night as John Paul Jones and Kiki Dee let rip with Julie rehearsing 'Hard Rain'. You don't forget nights like that.

Every picture tells a tale #7589

I'm looking at fading photos that tell several tales, some of which are repeatable. That's Julie Felix who is the reason we started Mighty Quinn Management. I was working as a producer for the South Bank Show documentary TV series and suggested we do a programme on the Folk boom of the Sixties that took Folk Music into the Folk Rock movement. Julie had been a big part of the period in the UK when she was showcased by David Frost on his TV series 'The Frost Report'. She went on to have allsorts of hits followed by 3 series of her own show on BBC2 TV featuring the finest artists of the Sixties.

I thought it would be a good idea to track Julie down in the Nineties and make the documentary through her eyes and focus. She was attempting to make a comeback at that time, having lived outside the UK for many years, but she had an agent/manager who was a dope. He was putting her out into ghastly little venues for peanuts.. Nuts! This was a truly gifted performer/singer/songwriter. After hearing this agent tell Julie he was the cog at the centre of the showbiz wheel (cock would have been nearer the mark), I told her she needed better management. Dispirited, she blazed, "So manage me!" That was the last thing on my mind. I contacted many friends in showbiz asking them if they knew of a good agent or manager. They all replied in the same way: "There's no such thing!"

And so it came to pass that I sat down at a desk and started phoning venues to see if I could place a worthwhile tour for Julie. It wasn't particularly easy. A lot of venues had been taken over by councils and councillors were now handling bookings.

These are people who shouldn't be anywhere near the world of entertainment. Also, there were a lot of young people in charge of venues who had never heard of Julie. This I found intolerable as if you are working in the business you should have an interest and knowledge of what has gone down before yesterday. However, bit by bit I warmed to the job and put in place a 40 date tour of the UK, hitting very nice theatres and art centres. As I became the cock at the centre of the wheel it came naturally to me to judge just how far I could push the fee upwards at each venue. It doubled and then tripled, heading ever skyward.

Next came the promotion. Well that proved to be easy when I realised that Julie's TV series had helped the careers of many big names back in the Sixties. It was time to Godfather up and call in those favours. We masterminded a new double album of Dylan tracks for Julie, bringing in members of Led Zeppelin and other names. Suddenly Julie's name was back where it belonged. She was all over that modern wonder, the internet. The album was launched at the first concert of the tour and sold a bundle each night. The tour packed them in. I went along as manager, roadie, friend, head of merchandise table and clockwatcher. It was a blast. After each gig we would head to the hotel for a Becks or 3 and I would empty my pockets of hundreds of pounds in sales. That bit topped off each day very nicely.

And so Mighty Quinn Management was launched. And yes, that is Donovan in the photos at his Surprise 60th Birthday Party that we organised. But that's another tale…

Julie Felix – In the Beginning and
After the End

I was visited by Julie Felix 4 hours after she died last night. Her presence filled my office. We didn't speak. There were many unresolved issues between the two of us. They were so unresolved you could say they were resolved. But it wasn't always that way. We'd loved each other once. A lot.

As a teenager back in 1966 I certainly loved her. I enjoyed the Two Ronnies and John Cleese but it was Julie I turned on for each week on The Frost Report. That coy smile at the end of each song got me. She was definitely a Sixties Sex Bomb for this muppet of a Catholic schoolboy. Her first LP was played LOUD as I lay with the cover in my hands gazing adoringly at the shining hair and sallow skin of this Mexican/Californian Goddess. 'Deportees' is still the sexiest protest song I've ever heard. The months moved on and Julie was the star of her own BBC TV series featuring the finest selection of guests from the era. She started writing her own songs and they were fabulous. She was huge, man! And then she disappeared.

Nearly 25 years later I suggested to Melvyn Bragg that we do a South Bank Show documentary on the folk boom of the 1960s. He agreed that was worth looking back at and so I started scrawling notes to take the show from Jimmy Hall and Robin McGreggor to Dylan and Donovan. And then, while flicking through a newspaper from Devon (don't ask), I saw a tiny advert proclaiming that Julie Felix would be playing The Black Grape pub just off Dartmoor. Holy Moley! Jane and I headed out. It was a crappy pub in the back of beyond. Julie was changing in the Ladies toilet. The show was fabulous. The audience not so.

We met Julie after the show and we got on instantly with a lot of laughter. The South Bank Show didn't come off for whatever reason but Felix and the Quinns kept in touch. Turned out her agent was an asshole. We sat in on one meeting with him. He described himself as the cog at the centre of the Mighty Wheel of Showbiz and Julie was a mere spoke. Cock rather than cog would have been a more apt description. I said so to Julie over a coffee later. This irritated her as you have to have faith in your agent. "Well if you think you can do a better job, do it!" she raged/pleaded. I didn't think this would be particularly difficult as the cock had been putting Julie into horrible little venues around the country. However, I first put word out to my friends in the business to ask if they knew of a good agent or manager that might be more suitable. The same answer came back from everyone: "No such thing as a good agent!"

And so early one morning I found myself sitting at my desk with phone in hand talking to theatres and Art Centres across the UK attempting to sell Julie Felix. The hardest bit would be that I often found myself talking to young bookers who had never heard of her. "She was with Dylan at the Isle of Wight," I would boast. "Oh no, we don't want anything like that," declared one meathead. I couldn't have got Bob the gig that day. "Julie who?" asked another backstage pudding. "The name means nothing to me. You do realise we have the Backyard Beatles here next week? They pack 'em in." Fucking tribute acts were becoming the order of the day even over the original artists themselves. But I persevered while grinding my teeth to the gums. We ended up with a 40 date tour in beautiful venues across the UK. And the fee? I'd initially plucked a figure from thin air and kept increasing it as each venue accepted my offer. It was already 4 times more than the cock had been getting for her. There's a lot of bullshit involved in selling an artist no matter how good they might be. I found this came naturally to me for which I'm thankful to the Irish Christian Brothers at my old school and the masterminds who were running Marvel Comics during my tenure there.

Julie, Jane and I made a good working team covering all aspects of selling, promoting, a life on the road, and performance. We were her agents/managers and roadies. Julie's daughter preferred the term slaves. On that first tour we had a blast after a few problems were ironed out. Julie's naturally scatty approach was to leave at the last possible moment to ensure a mad panic to get to each venue before curtain up. After the first month I put my foot down to my teenage heartthrob and insisted we left in so much time that she would be able to have a couple of hours chilling out in her dressing room before hitting the stage. As I was the one bringing in the gigs and my demands were light, she agreed to this and even started to enjoy it. She was always at her best after a couple of Beck's, straight after a successful show. And they were successful. Bottle in hand she would start to open up as we sat in the hotel room counting money from merch sales. And what tales she told of glorious encounters in the Sixties. Pissing off McCartney. Loving Dusty. David Frost in a lift. Her time on a Greek island with Leonard Cohen. Dylan.

A tour moment comes to mind: Julie was speeding down a motorway at 120 mph. I mentioned that was the speed Princess Diana had been travelling at the end. Next second we hit a pea soup fog bank. Brakes applied. As we came to a halt, we heard the screech of brakes from a car speeding towards us from behind. Brace ourselves and WOOOMPH! When we came to a stop, I looked at Julie and she looked at me. Her first words were: "The guitars!" They were in the boot behind us, including her precious Martin. Happily they survived and, of secondary importance, so did we.

It would be true to say Julie was careful with her money. I think she was conscious of having had it once upon a time and then not having had it. Now she was making a fair amount once again out on the road. She was keen to keep as much of it as possible and so we would sometimes share a hotel room if, as was normal, the venue hadn't booked us one as part of the fee deal. Bed time involved a few bizarre yoga moves in her pyjamas followed by a chant or three to the Goddess of the moment.

She did love us, of that I'm sure. For a while. We had given her a self-belief in her abilities once again. Put her back on a map. No more changing in ladies toilets. She was very grateful and even went so far to kiss me passionately late one night when she was in her cups. It was my birthday, the day she scrawled the message in this picture. She pushed me up against the wall inside her deserted house and the kiss lingered beyond the normal accepted artist/manager peck. It was a strange moment considering my sexuality. It was a particularly strange moment for the teenage me who had collected her LP's. Like a good journalist (remember them?), I made my excuses and left.

The tour worked. It was a success. We made money. The venues made money. The audience was entertained. "Let's do it again!" said Julie, on a high at tour's end. Back on the phones. Jane and I then had the rather brilliant idea of producing a brand new double album with Julie covering Dylan's lifetime of songs. And we suggested she ask some of her friends from the Sixties to back her on the 'Starry Eyed and Laughing' double CD. In came Led Zeppelin's John Paul Jones on mandolin, Kiki Dee and John Renbourn amongst others. This was fun, especially when JPJ turned up for an Easter egg hunt at Julie's and the day ended up with a jam. Possibly the best ever version of Hard Rain Gonna Fall, especially when it morphed into No Regrets.

The album sold well as did the following 40 date tour, which we assumed would be the last as Julie was by now well into her sixties. But she was having a ball and didn't want the show to end. She encouraged us to start booking another tour and to open up as Mighty Quinn Management and work with other acts. We put this off for a while as working with just Julie took up 24 hours each day. But word had spread that we were that oxymoron: Good agents. And soon we took on a few more acts and found each day could hold 48 hours or more. This worked for a while but it soon became obvious that Julie regretted the decision to bring in other artists to our tiny roster. The prima donna in her demanded our full attention. I think there was a fear inside for her of slipping back to agent cock status. We trundled on for a few more years with Jane masterminding huge charity concerts and TV appearances for Julie (back with David Frost again after nearly 40 years!), alongside on-going tours. And then one day Julie said she had heard that we had approached a festival offering them herself but only if they also took one of our other acts, an Australian singer. This was utter nonsense and we told her so. But she had her doubts which irritated me as much as it irritated her. Jane got the festival organiser himself to call Julie and say this hadn't happened but a rot had set in to our relationship. Little things became big. Drip…drip…drip. Sad really. One thing led to another and we parted company acrimoniously.

We didn't speak again. She played Liverpool a couple of times in the last few years but I couldn't be the bigger man and get up the enthusiasm to go. And so we didn't talk…..until last night. But even then she was newly dead and I still didn't have the words. But her presence was very evident. She always had great stage presence….even in death. Of course, I'm sad that things ended as they did but still cheesed by the little things. That's being stupidly human, I guess. Damn the little things! In truth I do hope that Julie is starry eyed and laughing today up amongst the Goddesses. There is so much more to our story but I shall happily let it fly to the heavens.

Concert

A Mighty Quinn Production with John Paul Jones of Led Zeppelin and Roy Harper. Here we are backstage at rehearsal for a bonzo show in aid of landmine clearance. Bill Wyman and his Rhythm Kings were also on the bill.

We were managing Julie Felix who we had hosting the show. For the grand finale she chose a Lennon song, which she assumed everyone knew. Nobody did. They had all assumed it would be Give Peace a Chance. It wasn't. It was 'Bring on the Lucie'. So the finale ended with everyone on stage clutching sheets with the words to this wonder song as the lyric was passed from Kiki Dee to Bill Wyman to Georgie Fame to Steve Harley to John Paul Jones to Albert Lee to ...

It worked. These were professionals and this was a Lennon song.

Dream Girls

Back in 1965, I carefully cut out of Melody Maker newspaper and pinned up on my bedroom wall next to Cilla. Two beautiful girls. A 12 year-old could dream, couldn't he? Judith Durham of the Seekers and Julie Felix, protest singer of note. Cut ahead from 1965 to 2002. Jane and I are running Mighty Quinn Management and Julie was our first signing and dear friend. One day in Chelsea we find ourselves in a coffee shop sitting opposite Julie and Judith Durham. As they chat about days long gone and tours to come, I sit back and take in the pair. They still have that Sixties magic that had them branded as part of the Beautiful People. I can't resist telling them that they once shared my bedroom wall with Cilla (and Lady Penelope). They are suitably flattered after the initial laughter. I can't remember what we ate with our coffee but I do remember I had a big 12 year-old's daft smile on my face throughout. The girls were alive and buzzing and I trust that they are both still so and happily touring the cosmos with their unforgettable music. Shining stars both.

A Moment in Time

The first tour Jane and I put in place for American folk singer Julie Felix covered over 40 dates across the UK. Heading up North for the Scottish leg of the tour, Julie suggested we take a diversion and walk along the Roman built Hadrian's Wall.

Once away from the motorway, we were soon stepping back to this all-important time in British history. It took little imagination to turn into Quinntus and Felicis as we wandered further and further along the ancient wall. Nothing had changed since Roman and slave had piled those bricks together. We felt the moment. And then the modern world crashed in without warning as a war plane screamed over head, forcing us to fall to our knees in instant terror. In a second it was gone, leaving our bones still rattling.

Memories of Stan Lee

Wandering around the Marvel offices with Stan one day in 1993 it seemed particularly crowded with editorial staff, directors and executive directors. I asked him about the early days of the creation of the Marvel Universe back in the early Sixties. "There were about six of us in the office back then. Just two on a good day. I don't know half the people here today. All I know is that I probably don't want to know most of them." As I was myself at this time involved with on-going battles with the Marvel Licensing Dept., I knew exactly what he meant.

Out to lunch with Stan Lee one day, he turned to me and asked the question: "So what is the greatest story ever told?" I wondered for a moment if Stan had been born again and the answer was going to have religious overtones. Interestingly, every illustrator I've ever worked with has expressed a desire to work on the Bible. Nothing to do with their beliefs but rather their natural artistic instinct for that most visual of stories. To my delight Stan's answer to the question was Jack and the Beanstalk. His reasons: "It's a story you never forget through your whole life from age two onwards. It's got the lot: a great flawed hero, ferocious villain, drama, comedy, and scenes that are so visual they remain imprinted on your imagination forever." I couldn't disagree with that, and indeed I went on to create many stories about Jack and his magic beans in my 'Blue Moon' comic book years later.

A year before his death, Stan heard that I was working on comic book literacy projects in schools across Merseyside for the children's charity Liverpool Heartbeat. He asked if I would like him to write an inspirational poem to go into one of these books. I'm sure you can imagine my answer. I've read the poem out at a zillion school assemblies ever since. I think everybody of every age should memorise the poem and recite it at the beginning of each day. Here it is for you, gentle reader.

TO BE A SUPER-HERO
By Stan Lee

You don't have to be
A super-hero
To make the world
A better place

You don't have to have
A super power
To do your bit
For the human race

You don't have to wear
A mask or costume
Or battle a bandit
Atop a runaway train

All you need to do
Is show compassion
Reach out your hand
To those in pain

You don't have to slay
A deadly dragon
You don't have to risk
Life or limb

You don't have to fight
An evil villain
You needn't do
Anything grim

158

It's really not hard
To be a hero
You can do it with ease
On your own

Just give your heart
To those who are ailing
Let them know
That they're not alone!

Over the years, whenever Stan wrote an editorial for my 'Exploits of Spider-Man' comic, he would always say: "If you don't like it, let me know and I'll try again." As if! Everything he wrote was always bang on the button. One day I suggested to him that it was time for his autobiography and maybe we could do a comic strip version. He liked the idea and suggested John Buscema as illustrator with me as the editor. John was definitely up for the job and we had many interesting conversations about capturing Stan's life from the Twenties onwards. Sadly, it was one of those projects that didn't get any further than our talks. But it is one hell of a book in my head!

The McCartney Tour

I liked Paul's brother from way back when he first popped up on the scene back in 1963, or was it 1964. It seemed very genuine that he had changed his name from McCartney to McGear so that it wouldn't seem as if he was trading on his big brother's fame as he entered the bright lights of showbiz. It would probably have been even more genuine if he hadn't held a press conference to let this fact be known. Anyway, I enjoyed his band, the Scaffold when they popped up on the wireless and telly. They kind of fitted in during the gap between the Goons and Monty Python. John Gorman was funny. Roger McGough was poetic. And Mike McGear was......Paul's brother. A fun band. Check them out on Youtube. I first met Mike sometime in the Seventies and we got on very well. He liked all things comic. On one day we sat down together and wrote a two page story for a proposed comic all about the Number Seven bus he and 'our kid' used to take on adventures across their childhood. "Well, that was a load of shit," he declared a short time later, and who am I to disagree?

Our paths crossed many times over the decades including at dear friend and 5th Beatle Derek Taylor's funeral wake in 1997. It was here that wife Jane mistook George Harrison for me and gave him my sandwiches and tea. By 2013 I had spent several years touring theatres and art centres across the UK with a one-man stage show of my devising telling the history of comic books and my own small part in it. Having played over 200 dates, I suggested to Mike that he put a similar show together about his own life. As he had been taking photos since birth and had already written his own autobiography, I felt that the stories and images were all in place to make for a highly entertaining show. He agreed and we decided to start the tour a year hence giving me good time to sell the idea to suitable venues and for him to cobble the storyline and Powerpoint presentation together. He told me that he was even going to buy a new car so that he could zip up and down the country in style. This type of show is the easiest to present as all you need to take with you is a memory stick carrying the images to the stories you are about to tell. What could possibly go wrong?

Mike agreed that he would have the show ready to test on a local audience in six months time, leaving the following six months to tinker with the show before starting the tour. By the time we reached that six month spot, Jane and I had already put in a 30 date tour of theatres and art centres across the land. Mike had yet to put pen to paper but that didn't concern me too much. He had his autobiography to ransack. It was one of the best books I've read on that period. I asked Mike if he wanted the venues to pay direct to him or whether he'd prefer the money to come direct to Mighty Quinn Management from which we would then pay him. He agreed to the latter to save him the hassle of having to then pay us. The first date of the tour was going to be playing the popular Pitlochry Festival up in Scotland.

But before that we had to fit in the trial show to test a friendly audience reaction. This finally came about two week's before the start of the tour at a local church hall on the Wirral. Two days before this, Mike started to put the show together. "Do you know how to do this Powerpoint thing?" he asked. Everything that could go wrong went wrong with his computer.

My mind boggled at the seeming lack of direction of the storyline he was attempting to capture. My mind boggled even more when I finally saw the show for the first time in the church hall a couple of days later. It was a friendly audience and thank God for that otherwise they should have lynched him. His script was non-existent. The stories he told all meandered to nothing. For example, up on the screen came a photo of Ivan Vaughan. "Oh yeah," says Mike. "That's Ivan. Shame what happened to him." And then he clicked on to the next photo and a new story.

No mention of just what happened to Ivan or the rather important fact that it was he or introduced John to Paul thereby kicking off the wonder of the age. I sat in my chair at the back of the church hall feeling more and more depressed. The show was bloody hopeless. Mike had had such an interesting life and he had captured none of it. I remember telling him that he should open the show with German planes bombing Liverpool as he was born and show the city in ruins, and close the show with a lovely photograph of himself in the White House with the Obamas to show how far he had travelled in this life. This didn't make it into the cut. After this first trial show, Mike's old bandmate John Gorman came up to me and asked: "So, Mr Quinn, what are you going to do about that?" I shook my head and asked: "What do you suggest, John?" "Don't worry, I'll have a word with him." This was a mighty relief, but news became quite grim during the following two weeks leading up to the tour proper.

Apart from in Liverpool and Scarborough, tickets simply weren't selling. In a nutshell, sales were diabolical. Mike wanted to know why this was. I told him that we had done everything we always do with the tours we put in place through Mighty Quinn Management. We had two tours in place at that time with Australian acts and ticket sales were excellent. As with all our tours we had got Mike interviews on all local BBC radio stations and local newspapers relating to tour dates. We had posters up across all towns and cities. This had always worked wonders up until now. 28 of our 30 dates simply weren't selling seats.

I suggested we cancel the tour but Mike wanted to forge ahead. "The show must go on, Timothy!" A few days later I was surprised/shocked/horrified/enraged to get a bill for several thousand pounds from a coach company for the hiring of a tour bus. Extra costs were added for painting the name 'Mike McGear McCartney' and the title of the tour, 'Sex, Drugs and Rock 'n' Roll (I wish!)' on both sides of the bus. I rang Mike to find out WTF. "The last time I was on tour my management company paid for my tour bus," he explained. "Who was your management company back then?" I asked. "Warner Brothers," said Mike. After a moment for this to sink in, I replied: "Mike,

162

you've been to our house. You know Mighty Quinn Management is me and the missus. We're not fucking Warner Brothers nor do we have any desire to be."

A day before we drove up to Pitlochry I was at Mike's house when the phone rang. As Mike chatted, it was obvious 'our kid' was on the line. When he hung up, I asked Mike what Paul had had to say about the tour. "Just one thing. He told me to remember whose name I've got." Interesting. I think I would have managed a 'good luck' if my own younger brother was heading out on tour. Pitlochry proved to be ok. Beautiful theatre and lovely crowd who were there for the festival and quite happy to spend 90 minutes in the company of a Beatle brother. Mike's pacing and storytelling ability was still bloody awful.

As the tour kicked off I found that Mike had contacted each venue to make sure that the fee was sent directly to him. This made me look a bit of a dope when I asked them to hand over the fee to me. I brought it up with Mike and told him that he would have to arrange to transfer part of that fee to our bank account. "I'm very busy at the moment," replied Mike. "When I've got some time I'll get round to it." A definite FU moment. I'd spent months setting up this tour and all promotions on good faith. I turned to Mike and said, "You know what, Mike. Forget it. Keep every penny." This was said rather than giving him a slap round the chops and to make him realise he was being an arse of the first order. But, serve me right, he took me at my word and either he's been incredibly busy over the last 8 years or he really is keeping every penny from the tour.

As the years went by Mike and I would occasionally cross paths in the village that is Liverpool. At one event I walked up to him and asked, "So can we laugh about it now, Mike?" He grimaced and turned on his heel and walked away in search of medicinal compound, so I guess not.

Supergirl's Sister Plays the Cavern Club

It was Ken Dodd who introduced me to Supergirl's sister. Ken, 'the funniest man in the universe', had been a constant in my life since childhood days when the whole family would gather round the telly to watch his Christmas specials. I first met him when I was seventeen at the City Varieties Music Hall where he played shows that went with the warning 'bring sandwiches and a flask'. Audiences would leave the theatre long after midnight, weak with laughter. And Ken was always very kind to the stagehands, never forgetting to give us a tip, which belies his reputation that he was very careful with his money. He was only careful whee the taxman was concerned. Back in Liverpool after 48 years, I would often bump into Ken. He would always greet me with a cheery, "Get your bloody hair cut! You'll never get anywhere in this business with hair like that!" As Ken's trademark mop top was as famed as John, Paul, George and Ringo's, this always raised a smile.

One day in 2016 he invited me to a party where he introduced me to the Headmaster of a local blind school. The Head invited me along to the school to attempt to create a brand new comic book with his students. Surprisingly this worked very well despite the obvious drawback. While at the school several of the pupils told me that there favourite TV series was 'Supergirl'. They were so excited about the show that I tuned in when I got home. The students' favourite character in the show was Supergirl's sister who was played by the actor Chyler Leigh who had previously starred in the hospital drama series 'Grey's Anatomy'. I thought it would be fun if I could attempt to get

Chyler to send a message to the pupils of the school so set about tracking her down on the net.

Five minutes after sending her an email, I got a reply asking: 'Can we Skype'. Five minutes after that I found myself face-to-face via computer screen with Chyler herself and her rock star husband Nathan West. Chyler explained that she often sang with Nathan's band, East of Eli. The two of them loved the idea of doing something for the kids of the blind school and asked me if I knew a suitable venue in Liverpool that they could come over to play a fund raising concert at. "What about the Cavern Club?" I suggested. Both Nathan and Chyler were blown away by such a thought. "You could get us the Cavern?!"

Thanks to Bill Heckle, the fabulous owner of the Cavern Club, this was set in stone after a single phone call. Bill is one of the great guys who has done so much for Liverpool over the last few decades. A fabulous businessman with a golden heart. The show was a huge success and complete sellout. Chyler invited the school choir on stage to sing a number with her. The song was the Beatles classic 'Blackbird'. Chyler choked on the line 'Take these sunken eyes and learn to see'. My friend from Marvel days, Alan Cowsill, was in the audience and described the night as "the most moving concert I've ever been at." And Alan has been at a lot of concerts! After the show Chyler and Nathan set up a Meet & Greet which went on until five in the morning. I have to say that the Cavern Club staff were very understanding about this unexpected all-nighter. Bless them all. Chyler found the whole night highly emotional, especially when I introduced her to Len Garry, one of John Lennon's original Quarrymen. To top things off, Bill came to me at the end of the night with a huge bulging bag of takings for the event. Every night should end like that.

Jeffrey Archer, Sir Tim Rice
and Jeremy Paxman

Having spent a great portion of my career interviewing people (Google 'Tim Quinn and Katy Manning' on Youtube for an example) , this was a talent I wanted to pass on to the next generation when I started producing workshops in schools. To this end I would spend a term with prospective journalists guiding them in the simple art of research and question forming before setting up interviews with major names. One of my favourites for these school interviews was the day I took four children down to London to meet acclaimed author Jeffrey Archer.

The children ranged in ages from 9-14. Jeffrey had invited us to interview him at his penthouse pad overlooking parliament. The penthouse was beyond spectacular and had the very best views in London. Jeffrey was in fine form and had arranged a splendid spread of cakes and biscuits for the students to relax with before going into interview mode. He invited each student to go and chose a book for him to sign from his office. The interview went swimmingly and Jeffrey didn't even raise an eyebrow when one of the nine year-olds asked: "This is a beautiful place you live in, so what was it like to go from this into prison?" Without a pause, Jeffrey answered, "I'll tell you what it was like, young man. It was dreadful You don't want to go into prison!" After the interview and photos, we took the private elevator down to the ground floor. As we stepped outside, the school rang us to say that Jeffrey was already tweeting about us. Happily the tweet was highly favourable of the students and their school.

Sir Tim Rice was an equal delight when he invited my students along to his beautiful home in Barnes. We ended the day feeding his chickens in the garden. As I was about to leave, Sir Tim slipped me a cheque for £500 to help with printing costs for the school magazine in which the interview would appear.

I took another group of students to interview that master political inquisitor Jeremy Paxman between filming episodes of his 'University Challenge' series. Having watched many of Jeremy's political interviews on line, the students were understandably nervous at facing the man himself. This all changed when he greeted us with a huge platter of sandwiches and the invite to tuck in. The following interview went well until we reached the question: "All you need is love?" He blinked and stuttered, "What?! You can't ask me that!" When I pointed out that that answer was actually very telling, he smiled and nodded in agreement, "I suppose it is, you devils!"

I only had one name turn me down for a school interview. That was a man called Michael Gove who at that time was the Education Secretary in the government. "Will the interview be national?" he asked. "It will appear in the school magazine," I replied. "Oh no. I'm far too busy for that." Need I say more.

Dustin Hoffman

"Just one word. Plastics. There's a great future in plastics. Nuff said."

When I walked into the flix to see The Graduate that day back in 1968 I had no idea it would be a movie I would watch with sheer delight countless times through my life. Jane too over in Indiana, USA. For me I was just passing time that afternoon while playing truant. Took about 5 minutes into the story for me to get into the groove. I had about as much idea of the direction my life was taking as Benjamin, although, again like him, I knew I wanted to avoid the plastics. Dustin Hoffman became an acting hero that afternoon.

Cut ahead about 34 years and imagine our delight when Jane and I find ourselves hanging around on a film set inside Richmond Theatre gabbing with the man himself. Dustin is there to make the theatre scenes from the movie Finding Neverland, the story of JM Barrie's first production of Peter Pan. Barrie was played by Johnny Depp. It's a fairly simple scene they were concentrating on that afternoon. About 20 lines shared between them. We watched as they performed the scene 32 times. Absolutely fascinating. Between each take, Dustin would come back and chat with us. The main part of the conversation I remember now was about an accident he had had with a deckchair the day before when he had managed to slice off a finger. He was full of good humour about the incident and even more praise for how the nurses and doctors at the local hospital had rallied round. While he chatted with us, Johnny stayed aloof over in a corner, still obviously in character. I remember that with each take, Depp played it exactly the same while Dustin would alter both his delivery and movements, and on the word CUT his character would be dropped and he would head back over to us, smiling. He was having fun while Johnny was at work. And as for me, I somehow smothered my urge to ask Dustin to bellow the name ELAINE as loud as he could while hammering on a nearby glass window.

John Hurt

Really should be used to everybody shuffling off this mortal coil after last year, but, in the words of Paul McCartney, it is a real drag to hear of John Hurt's departure. Back in 1967 I went to see 'A Man for All Seasons' and absolutely loved his performance as Richard Rich. It was a fairly minor character in the story but he was magic. So much so that I stayed in my seat and watched the movie twice that day. AND I came back the following day to see it again. Initially, I had mistaken John for the actor Alfred Lynch who had played Hereward the Wake in a favourite telly series of mine earlier in the decade.

The years ticked on as they have a nasty habit of doing and suddenly it was 1999. I was down in London with Gillian Baverstock, the elder daughter of Enid Blyton, to launch our publishing company. We were giving interviews at Gillian's club off Sloane Square. I suddenly heard a very familiar voice approaching. It was the unmistakable tone of John Hurt. He was there with his agent to discuss upcoming work. He apologised when he realised he had interrupted our interview. He and the agent sat at a distance but were obviously tuned in as we restarted filming.

Half an hour later as we were leaving the room, John smiled up at me and said, "Enid Blyton? I've always loved Enid Blyton." Golden opportunity. "And I've always loved your performance as Richard Rich," I replied. He laughed. "That is going back a bit."

Later that afternoon, I was sitting on my own in the club bar when John came over to me with the words: "Do you mind if I join you?" Caught off guard, I could think of no reason to turn away this most marvellous of actors, and so we spent the afternoon chatting on everything from children's fiction to Marvel Comics, old time Music Hall, movies and the stage.

"Do you mind if I join you?" I shall never forget those words. Thanks for joining me, John. Never forgotten.

Always Comics

It's funny what can develop from a simple comic book. I've always loved the medium of telling stories in pictures. The cavemen got it right when they decided to pick up their knuckles from the ground and start daubing slop on their cave walls. The stories they created are still communicating with us all these years later. For the last few years I have been creating brand new comic books for the Merseyside based children's charity Liverpool Heartbeat.

These comics are placed into schools across the region to lure non-readers via exciting pictures and accompanying words into the world of literacy. I have a fabulous team of illustrators I work with from the worlds of DC Comics, Marvel Comics, the Beano, and children's picture books. These are Russ Leach, Lew Stringer, Nigel Parkinson, Holly Bushnell and George Sears. Be sure to check out their work all over the internet. The first comic book we produced told the story of John Hulley, a forgotten Liverpudlian who back in the 1860s organised the first modern day Olympic Games.

The comic book raised awareness of this man to such an extent that a statue in his honour has since been erected with Princess Anne doing the honours at the unveiling. It was a very surreal moment as I stood on the banks of the River Mersey shaking hands with the Princess who told me she particularly enjoyed page 11 in the comic book!

In 2022, we produced a comic book for Liverpool Heartbeat telling the life story of Her Majesty Queen Elizabeth II. This was to celebrate her Platinum Jubilee. The comic went into a zillion schools in celebration. I'm happy to say that the Queen commented favourably on the comic and was very happy to see her grandchildren enjoying reading it. She even gave Liverpool Heartbeat the treasured Queen's Award for Voluntary Service. The comic is now available from Phoenix Press. It was a truly remarkable tale to tell and each of my artists captured the periods from the 1920s to the present day so well.

And in the End

When I first was asked to write my autobiography back in 2015, the publisher suggested I stick mainly to the comic book stuff. That was easy enough. This time around I was cleared to shove in the rest. But what is the rest? I mean, I've always wanted this book to be above all things entertaining. But some memories while moving and heartfelt to me are surely pointless observations to anyone else. Case in point this very morning when my elder brother Michael Zooms in from Oz. As usual we reminisce about days long gone. "You've got to put in that day we bought the rocket ship back in 1958," he suggests. We then spent the next five minutes flying back in time. "Remember it operated on simple water pressure via a hand pump. We took it out onto the lawn and pumped away for dear life. It must have shot 100 feet into the air leaving a glorious plume of water behind it. That was the true Space Age!" For one brief shining moment we had been transported back to that glorious moment in our lives. We could feel the thrill and the energy and the sheer joy of being 5 and 10 years of age in the year 1958. Well, there you go. The last paragraph was for my brother. Apologies to any other reader.

Mugged

I've been mugged. Twice. Once in Liverpool back in 1980. Talk about a mug! I was coming out of a bank counting one hundred pounds in five pound notes. Two youths approached me and suggested I hand the money over. I laughed. I actually laughed. It was broad daylight in a busy street. Why this was daylight robbery! They didn't take kindly to my laughter and one of them pulled a knife from what seemed to be his underpants. "Hand it over!" I hadn't been threatened with a weapon since my schooldays under the Irish Christian Brothers and their merciless straps. "Get lost!" I said, or words to that effect. The next thing I knew the footpad had stabbed me in my left shoulder. Blood actually spurted out. They grabbed the money and legged it. I fell to the ground in a blue funk trying to figure out how far away from my heart the knife wound had been driven. I was wearing a white shirt that was transformed into red in mere moments. I thought my time was up. Panic all around me. Police arrive. The wound is looked at and they declare, "It's just a scratch. You'll be all right." A scratch! I had convinced myself I was almost dead. "Will you catch the bastards?" I asked. Both policemen laughed. They didn't. For the next six months I slipped into a rather glum mood. I will not use the word depression because that is a completely different kettle of fish that everybody and their dog lay claim to these days, but I was definitely glum, chum. And then one day I woke up and thought, "Why am I feeling so down?" It was, of course, because somebody had stabbed me. Okay, scratched me. But then I thought back to the two Scouse halfwits with the knife. The simple realisation made me smack myself hard in the chops in disgust. I was buggered if I was going to let those two bloaters make me feel glum. The mood changed instantly and I've been this shining beam of light ever since.

Mugging 2 happened in a dark street in Nashville. I was there as a producer for TV's 'South Bank Show' making a documentary on women in Country Music. We'd had a great day filming and we were way ahead of schedule. At midnight I was wide awake and buzzing. I took off for a walk across town. I didn't realise I had crossed the line into the wrong side of town until a car drew up alongside me and four rednecks started a conversation. "Hey, faggot! Whatcha doin'?" I realised I was doomed as I looked down at my flowery shirt and knew my trademark flowery locks were blowing in the wind. I made the mistake of talking back. "Just out for a walk." My fruity accent was all they needed. The car stopped and they climbed out. One of them had a cudgel. The others didn't need cudgels. I don't know how many times I was hit but by the time I was on the sidewalk I remember picturing myself in a body bag. But, the next second they jumped back in the car and roared away. As I sat spluttering on the ground, a police car slowly drove by. The rednecks had obviously spotted it and taken to the hills. The cops didn't spot me however and drove on by. I sat there for a while blubbering to myself before common sense told me to get the hell away from there before my assailants drove round the block to finish the job. This time round I did not feel glum after the attack. Just sore. Mighty sore.

Rolling Stone

Backstage after another concert with Bill Wyman, late of the Rolling Stones. Mary Wilson of the Supremes has recently vacated Bill's lap. Georgie Fame sits in the far corner of the dressing room grumbling that the band had played more bum notes than ever before and that it had been a crap show. It most certainly hadn't been. The joint was a'rocking if Georgie wasn't. Bill is wearing a comedy t-shirt showing four playing cards and the words: 'FOUR KING GREAT!' Knowing Jane of old and that she was one of the few people left on this planet who has never sworn in her whole life, Bill took great delight in asking her to read the slogan. She did, slightly nonplussed. 'Say it again but faster,' instructed Bill. She did and it clicked. For Bill it was the funniest thing he'd heard that night. Even Georgie smirked. Jane, that innocent Fishers, Indiana girl had finally sworn thanks to one of England's most notorious old rockers. Bill couldn't have been prouder.

Martin Luther – Role Model

They do say that the Sixties didn't begin until 1963, but I recall that the times they were a'changing as early as Spring 1962. That was the time that my brother Michael and I saw a BBC TV drama about Martin Luther. We were radicalised on the spot and immediately became born again heretics. For the past decade we had suffered under the oppressive weight of the Catholic Church, being sent to convent and Irish Christian Brother schools where religious study was beaten into us with a Medieval zeal. All this and church on Sunday. To make matters worse, our local church was directly across the road from our house where a statue of St Joseph over the main doorway kept a stoney eye on our comings and goings. Earlier in the 1950s we had accepted the faith as fact and just a part of the trials of life as we made our way to Purgatory. But by the 1960s we started to question……everything.

Martin Luther and his Reformation appealed to us as would-be revolutionaries. We set to work on our own 95 theses or disputation on the power of the church. I think we got down about ten, which seemed enough. Our quibbles were mostly about the Catholic Catechism and over-long prayers. I do remember coming up with a line that read: 'The Word is Love'.

I was over the moon a few years later when the Beatles confirmed this Quinn fact on their Rubber Soul LP. We decided to get up at one o'clock in the morning to nip across the road and nail our proclamation to the right hand door you can see in this picture. We didn't put our names to the tract but rather signed off as 'The People'. While we had no fear of being

178

excommunicated, we felt extermination was more likely from our local priest. So, did it do any good? Well, does any revolution do any good? Count me out/in. It was certainly a fun moment in our time. A short while later we read up a little more on Martin Luther and found that he was a total arse, so a lesson was learnt. Don't follow leaders and watch the parking meters.

They do say that once a Catholic always a Catholic. I do believe that Michael and I are the exceptions to that rule.

Yesterday

1956 was a great year for fireworks in our house. In the weeks leading up to the 5th of November, brother Mike and I had collected a big box of Rip-Raps, Bangers, Sparklers, Roman Candles, Catherine Wheels, Pyramids, and Rockets. We kept the box between our beds, and, each day, we'd sit in front of the hissing gas fire and handle the gaily coloured mini bombs.

A favourite trick was to snap open two Bangers and lay a trail of gunpowder across the floor of our garage, just like we'd seen in various cowboy shows. The garage was a safe place because it was lined with asbestos. I remember my nails being clogged with a deadly mix of gunpowder and iron filings from our Chemistry Set, which had ended up in the garage along with a fascinating tin of quicksilver that bubbled swiftly in every direction on release. Oh, the joy of deadly danger as a boy!

HG Wells, GB Shaw and my Grandfather

My Quinn grandfather caused quite a stir when he formed the first non-sectarian choir at Liverpool's old cathedral nearly 100 years ago. He was the choir master and a Socialist of note. Through his political meanderings he met HG Wells and George Bernard Shaw who were visitors to the Quinn family home where discussions on the state of the common man were to the forefront. Hard to believe from their writings but these two were also Socialists from birth. Both Wells and Shaw tried to convince my Grandfather to stand for election as they recognised his general decency, soul and heart. Happily for the Quinn family, Laurence James Quinn had more sense than to enter that thrice poxed world and remained a happy man through his life.

And Today

As I await to turn 70 years of age, I find myself linked back to all the things I loved as a child. Second childhood? Surely it must be my 7th childhood by now? I'm currently curating a comic book section for the Liverpool Beatles Museum run by Roag Aspinall Best and his brother Pete. Music and comics. That'll do. I'm also still turning out brand new comic books for the children's charity Liverpool Heartbeat. Our aim with these comic books is to instil a love of reading in children. That'll do. And I'm also writing for the fabulous Phoenix Press children's imprint of New Haven Publishing to who I would like to say "thank you very much".

About the Author

It was a rainy day on a planet known as the 1980s. It rained a lot in the 80s where I waited for my shining knight to appear. And then, out of the blue, there he was. Where he came from, I do not know, but he did not arrive on a white steed. Instead he was hand delivered to my door on a white piece of ruled a4 paper by a postman wearing his summer uniform of short pants and safari hat. I fell in love instantly. (with Tim not the Postie.) it wasn't long before he asked me to spend "the rest of my lives" with him. (Tim not the Postie.) It is suddenly almost 40 years and several lifetimes later, and still we live and love and laugh. Are we not the two luckiest specks of stardust in the entire universe?
JANE QUINN

Titanic Tim
STAN LEE

Genius!
GYLES BRANDRETH

Tim Quinn is good for vibes!
BRIAN MAY

Please take this as your first warning. Three such warnings will result in dismissal.
PAUL NEARY

Lightning Source UK Ltd.
Milton Keynes UK
UKHW050623280223
417777UK00011B/197

9 781912 587797